THE JUDO TEXTBOOK
IN PRACTICAL APPLICATION

by Hayward Nishioka & James R. West

To Mr. and Mrs. Shigeru Egami,
Mr. and Mrs. Thomas E. Hunt, and to our fellow judoka.

©Ohara Publications, Incorporated 1979
All rights reserved
Printed in the United States of America
Library of Congress Catalog Card Number: 78-65737
ISBN 0-89750-063-6
Twelfth printing 1997

WARNING

OHARA Ⓘ PUBLICATIONS, INCORPORATED
SANTA CLARITA, CALIFORNIA

Preface

THE JUDO TEXTBOOK, a comprehensive manual for the beginning judoka, differs from Ohara's other how-to manuals by being much more than a picture book. While it does contain the customary techniques section, additional text has been devoted to auxiliary training methods, guidance in how to plan competitive strategy, a discussion of the International Judo Federation's recently updated rules and a thorough coverage of judo history and philosophy.

Laid out in a clear, straightforward manner, its format is similar to numerous history and social science textbooks, and for that reason we feel that it should be accessible to students from junior high through college. Amply supplied with information and rich in anecdote, each chapter is followed by a series of suggestions and practical applications. Two brief review quizzes follow each chapter. The **Test Yourself** quizzes encourage the student to reread the material not thoroughly understood in the first reading and also serve to provide topics for class discussion. The **True or False** questions are intended to assist the instructor in devising whatever is deemed necessary in the way of periodic written tests.

Coauthors Hayward Nishioka, fifth-degree black belt, and Jim West, second-degree black belt, are to be congratulated on their excellent overview of sport judo. They have fashioned an ideal textbook by taking the reader slowly but thoroughly through the basics and planting him considerably down the road toward achieving a black belt.

Although much of the material that has gone into the preparation of *The Judo Textbook* has appeared in articles Mr. Nishioka wrote for BLACK BELT magazine, he has ordered, supplemented with photographs, revised and expanded on earlier writings to present the beginning judoka with a broad, clear view of the sport, science and art of judo.

Aside from an excellent account of judo history, and along with rare biographical information about the founder of judo, Dr. Jigoro Kano, authors Nishioka and West provide detailed descriptions of the all-important falling techniques. Having duly emphasized the importance of mastering the science of falling, the reader is then given a step-by-step approach to learning 15 of the most basic

throwing techniques, five methods of pinning and five choke holds.

But perhaps most importantly, *The Judo Textbook* provides not only a detailed picture of judo past and present, but painstakingly imparts much of the unique flavor of the judo world. Clarifying myths and illuminating misconceptions without being preachy, the authors sustain an inspired and inspiring tone throughout.

Shag Okada
6th-Degree Black Belt
Coach of the 1974 and '75
U.S. International Judo Team

About the Authors

A member of the BLACK BELT Hall of Fame both as a competitor and as an instructor, Hayward Nishioka has compiled a brilliant record. Born in Los Angeles in 1942, none would have thought that he would eventually become one of America's premier judoka and a ranking black belt in karate. Beginning at the age of 12 he had his first lessons from his stepfather, Dan Oka. Dressed in an impromptu gi consisting of an old Army jacket, he was first put through the paces on a hardwood floor.

As a competitor his credits include the winning of the coveted 1967 Pan-American Games Gold Medal, the 1965 United States AAU National Grand Championship, the National Championships in 1965, '66 and 1970, fourth place in the World Championships 1967, selection to four All-American teams and he was a member of four United States International teams. As a karateka, he studied under internationally known karate master Tsutomu Ohshima and won the 1965 Nisei Week Karate Championships. More recently, he was the 1978 men's nage-no-kata National Champion and also the 1978 National Masters Champion in the 189-pound division. In addition, he was voted 1978 Coach of the Year by the National Collegiate Judo Association.

In the administrative area of judo, Mr. Nishioka has done much to promote the growth of judo. He is the founder and first president of the Southern California Collegiate Judo Conference,

Founder and Director of Camp Kodokan, a national summer camp for hard-core judo training. He is also a member of the Board of Directors of the Southern California Judo Association. Concerned with the schism in judo, he is a life member of both the United States Judo Association and the United States Judo Federation. Lastly, the author is an accredited National Referee.

Although receiving most of his judo training in the United States, Mr. Nishioka took two years out of his life to devote to serious training in Japan. At the age of 19, he traveled to Nara, Japan, where he practiced at Tenri University under the famous Yasuichi Matsumoto, the 6-foot-4 first All-Japan Champion. Spending one year at Tenri and another at the famed Kodokan Judo Institute in Tokyo, Japan, he gained much knowledge of the technical aspect of judo. While a special student at the Kodokan, he was honored along with James Bregman, another famous judoka, as being the first foreigners to demonstrate the nage-no-kata, the formal throw of judo, in the 1961 All-Japan Judo Championships. Concurrently, he studied shotokan karate under the direct disciple of Gichin Funakoshi, Master Shigeru Egami.

Upon his return to the United States, the author sensed a need to complete his education. Embarking on the path of knowledge, he received his Associate of Arts degree from Los Angeles City College. Diligently persisting at the California State University at

Los Angeles, he completed not only his Bachelor of Arts and Master of Arts in physical education but also finished a second Master's degree in administrative education.

Currently, Mr. Nishioka is an Associate Professor of physical education at Los Angeles City College, where he has done much to further the cause of the martial arts. At Los Angeles City College he has instituted one of the more extensive martial arts programs in the United States.

Drawing from his considerable knowledge of the martial arts, Hayward Nishioka has published extensively. Not only is he the author of *Foot Throws*, but also of over 100 articles that have appeared in BLACK BELT magazine and KARATE ILLUSTRATED. Added to this list are three martial arts films which he has produced and directed: *Nunchaku Exercises, Basic Judo* and *Personal Defense for Women*. And last but not least, he designed and produced two martial arts techniques charts as posters: "Basic Judo Techniques" and "Basic Karate."

———————

Born on October 11, 1945, James R. West had his first contact with judo at the age of seven. Briefly practicing as a child under Sensei John Ogden of Long Beach, California, he progressed rapidly. Unfortunately, James West's family moved to Lynwood, thus ending his practice of judo as a child. The seeds of contact sports, however, had been planted, and he pursued a different but related sport—wrestling.

In 1969, while attending California State University at Los Angeles, he met Hayward Nishioka. Mr. Nishioka had come to join the wrestling team, of which James West was the captain. From the beginning, the meeting was a mutually beneficial one. While teaching Hayward Nishioka the finer points of wrestling, he was, as he puts it, "somehow talked into entering a tournament in a sport which I thought I had forgotten all about." The tournament was the Oxnard Invitational. He defeated seven contestants in a row, was instantly promoted to brown belt and was forever after hooked on judo.

Practicing with the same avid devotion he had in wrestling, Mr. West's contest record in judo seemed to blossom. While still a

brown belt, Mr. West had defeated no less than six black belts and had placed in the Southern California District Championship as a brown belt. Receiving much of his instruction from former champions Gene LeBell and Hayward Nishioka, Mr. West was elevated to the rank of black belt within two years' time.

Completing his competition years in 1977, Mr. West's credits include being three times Southern California Open Division champion in judo, twice runner-up, and placing third in the 1975 National AAU Championships in the Open Division. He was also selected as an alternate on the 1975 United States Pan-American and World Games Judo Team. In the sport of sambo, he used much of his judo and wrestling skills to win first place in the 1975 AAU Sambo Championships. In sambo, he was a member of the 1975 and '77 world teams.

Completing his Master's degree in physical education in 1971, he did much of his work in the area of testing. Being somewhat of an expert in the area of testing, he undertook to test the personality differences of judoka and wrestlers for his Master's thesis. Presently, Mr. West is a physical education instructor at Haskell Junior High School in Cerritos, California. He is also a nightschool instructor at Cerritos College, where he founded the judo program. On the college scene, he is on the Board of Directors of the Southern California Collegiate Judo Association.

Contents

Chapter I

Introduction

Judo has sufficient scope and encompasses so many aspects of human culture that nearly every practitioner would define it's significance in personal terms. Moreover, judo is broad enough to accept as partly accurate, a wide variety of definitions. Judo is a sport, an art, a metaphysical science, a sort of spiritual involvement, a science of motion, a way of life and a science of self-defense. People come to judo for different reasons, and on staying, learn that judo fulfills a multiplicity of physical, mental and emotional needs.

The sportsman finds in judo a means of participating in a body contact sport which, though similar to wrestling, places more emphasis on standing and throwing techniques. The person seeking an effective means of self-defense discovers that a working knowledge of judo allows for the alternative of either disabling or controlling the aggressor. For the hyperactive, judo can be a form of catharsis, a means of channeling energy usefully. To the shy or withdrawn, judo can grant self-confidence.

Further, judo provides participants with a first-hand glimpse of a cultural and sporting activity through which another culture may be studied. The judoist learns the underlying reasons behind many of the obvious and subtle, if also sometimes stereotyped, mannerisms and customs associated with the Far East—for example, bowing, how it differs from handshaking.

But judo has its psychological, egocentric rewards, too. Participants find it exhilarating to have full control over an opponent while throwing him, and there is challenge to throwing while avoiding being thrown.

In that it stimulates both aerobic and anaerobic activity within the body, physical fitness and robust health are other sound reasons for practicing judo. In short, judo can provide the means for learning about and improving oneself—mentally, physically and psychologically.

PARTICIPATION IN JUDO IS WORLDWIDE

Encompassing many socio-economic strata, all ages and both sexes, participation in judo is truly global in scope. The last thoroughly official tally, to my knowledge—*Judo by the Kodokan*— listed approximately six million judoka in the world. That same census listed France as having 200,000 active judoka, a fact which at the time made France the most active judo-practicing nation outside the Orient. Although the United States was at that time listed as having 50,000 practitioners, a more recent survey conducted by BLACK BELT magazine's Yearbook in 1970 indicated a marked increase in the number of American participants, boosting the count to 135,000 judoka.

In 1961, Anton Geesink of Holland provided the West with an incentive by defeating Koji Sone of Japan to capture the World Judo Championship. This was the first time that a Caucasian had ever won the title. In 1964, Geesink again defeated the top Japanese contenders—only this time for a much bigger stake: the Olympic Gold Medal. The great Dutchman's feat did much to internationalize judo.

Although judo has many facets, recent trends have been toward increasing competition. The majority of people taking up judo today seem to plan to enter competitive tournaments. Be forewarned that those planning to attain such proficiency should be prepared to practice at least two or three times a week in two-hour sessions. National and international-level competitors work out at least three-to-five times a week with a minimum of two hours devoted to each session.

But the reader should not get the idea that competition is all there is to judo; in fact, it was the hope of the late Dr. Jigoro Kano, the founder of judo, that the practice of judo would instill certain lofty principles into the lives of judoka. Hoping to inspire more than physical vigor, Dr. Kano hoped that judo would be lived as a philosophy as well as being practiced as a skill.

DO'S AND DON'T'S IN LEARNING JUDO

1. Study the correct way of applying the throws. Throwing with brute force is not the correct way of winning in judo. The most important point is to win with technique.

2. First learn offense, and you will see that defense is included in offense. You will make no progress learning defense first.

3. Do not dislike falling. Learn the timing of the throw while you are being thrown.

4. Practice your throws by moving your body as freely as possible in all directions. Do not lean to one side or stiffen. A great deal of repetition in a throw will be rewarded with a good throw.

5. Increase the number of practices and contests. You will never make any progress without accumulating practice.

6. Do not select your opponents (which means do not say that you do or do not like practice with a certain person). Everyone has his own specialty. You must try to learn them all to make them your own.

7. Never neglect to improve the finer points. Practicing without any effort to improve will result in slow progress. Always recall your habits, as well as those of your opponent, while making improvement.

8. In practice, put your heart and soul into it. It will interfere with your progress in practice if you train without this spirit.

9. Never forget what your instructor or other higher-ranking members teach you. During practice you will make great progress if you keep in mind what they have said to you.

10. Try to continue your practice as much as possible. Training halfheartedly will result in a very grave setback to your progress.

11. Watch and study throws as much as possible when trying to improve and advance. The technique and mind are just like the front and back of one's hand, meaning they are very related.

12. Refrain from overeating and overdrinking. Remember that overeating and overdrinking will bring an end to your practice of judo.

13. Always try to think of improvement, and don't think that you are too good. The latter is very easy to do while learning judo.

14. There is no end to learning judo.

Translation of instructions given by
PROFESSOR YAMASHITA YOSHIAKI
10TH-DEGREE BLACK BELT, KODOKAN
Detroit Judo Club

PRACTICAL EXPERIENCE

Visit a number of judo schools or dojos (clubs) in your vicinity and note the different types of participation available. One should inquire if the school or dojo in question emphasizes sport judo, self-defense, exercise and character-building. Decide for yourself what you want out of judo; then attend the school offering the program that best suits your requirements.

TEST YOURSELF

1. List the several reasons for which one might practice judo.
2. Give the estimated number of judo participants throughout the world.
3. Name the first non-Oriental to win a major title in judo and list the titles won.
4. Briefly discuss the trend now prevailing in judo and what you think of it—good, bad or indifferent.
5. In keeping with this trend, what type of person would you say would be the most successful?
6. Discuss the difference between the amounts of time required of a person striving to improve himself, and the time needed by a person to train himself for national or international competition.
7. List at least 10 suggestions given by Professor Yamashita.

True-False Questions

1. Judo is not a body-contact sport.
2. Judo may be considered a recreational activity.
3. Judo is an anaerobic activity.
4. Anton Geesink of Holland was the first non-Oriental to win a world judo championship.
5. Geesink failed to win a gold medal in the 1964 Tokyo Olympics.
6. All judo schools follow the same lessons handed down by the Kodokan.

Chapter II

JUDO EQUIPMENT

Basically, there are three items necessary for the practice of judo—the dojo, the mat, the judo gi (pronounced *ghee*).

The dojo is not a gym, but rather a place which facilitates a better understanding of the self in relationship to one's peers.

To the Occidental way of thinking, a gym or a playing field is merely a place where one plays a game or sport—a place of utilitarian value only. Oriental martial artists, however, place a value on their practice halls that borders on reverence.

The word dojo translated means "the place to learn the way," and Orientals consider it a valuable place of many lessons where a practitioner may learn to master himself as well as his opponents. At the dojo, the judoist learns that in order to defeat an opponent, he must first control the little voice within him that says, "I can't," by replacing it with "I will." Here he is also taught respect for those who make his practice and knowledge of judo possible—from Dr. Kano, the founder, to his opponent or practice partner (without whom an increase in skill would be impossible). Surely, such a place deserves respect.

The dojo should be large enough to provide participants with room to move about freely and exercise their throws safely. The average dojo in the United States is roughly 30 feet by 50 feet (approximately 1,500 square feet) and accommodates up to 50 students per session. The largest dojo in the world is located in

Japan, where just one of its three rooms has an area of 9,000 square feet and accommodates up to a thousand participants at a time.

Proper care of the dojo is not done by physical means alone, though naturally the dojo must be kept clean. Maintenance is usually the responsibility of the practitioners, since they are the ones who benefit from its care; many students regularly arrive at practice sessions early in order to tend to the dojo. Physical care,

THE "KODOKAN"

however, is not enough. The student shows his gratitude for having a place to practice by bowing, both when he enters and leaves the dojo. The custom of bowing is discussed in Chapter III.

WHAT THREE TYPES OF MATS ARE USED IN THE UNITED STATES?

The most-preferred mats are the Japanese imported straw mats called *tatami*. They are usually three feet by six feet and are covered with vinyl. Although a little harder than most Americans are used to, they provide an excellent surface for the practice of judo.

The most common mat in American dojos is the packed saw-dust mat which is covered with stretched canvas. The principal advantage of this mat is that it is economical to construct. Secondly, its resiliency makes it more suitable for falling on.

Wrestling and gymnastics mats are also used. The gymnastics Ethofoam mats, when covered with canvas, are highly recommended for judo.

*THE JUDO GI IS THE UNIFORM WORN
BY ALL PRACTITIONERS OF JUDO*

Judo gi come in seven different sizes, ranging from size zero, suitable for five-year-olds, to size six, which should fit the average-sized pro-football lineman. There are three pieces to the judo gi: the jacket, pants and belt.

The jacket should fit comfortably about the participant and overlap left lapel over right. The sleeves of the jacket should extend to an area between the wrist and the mid-forearm.

Pants ought to be loose-fitting and long enough to cover the muscles of the calf. The strings along the side of the pants should be pulled snugly about the waist, placed through the loop and tied in a bow at the side.

Wrapped about the waist twice and tied in front in a square knot, the belt prevents the jacket from flapping about loosely, and presents a neat, tidy appearance. The judoka's degree of proficiency is represented by a different belt color—as will be explained in a later chapter.

Jacket and pants should be kept squeaky clean. Befitting the purity of judo, its heritage is enhanced by clean judo gi.

PRACTICAL EXPERIENCE

Visit a number of dojos to see their facilities and equipment. Note the overall condition of the room and mats. Try to visit during a practice and determine the degree of cleanliness of those actually involved in a workout. Do the participants seem to move about freely, or are much bumping and shuffling necessary due to overcrowding? Ask yourself whether or not you would like to practice at this dojo, and be prepared to justify why you feel as you do.

TEST YOURSELF

1. Name the three essentials necessary for practicing judo.
2. Explain the difference in thoughts as they relate to the dojo or gym—Occidental versus Oriental.
3. Explain what is meant by the statement, "The care of the dojo is not done by physical means alone."
4. List the three types of mats and their advantages or disadvantages.
5. Name the parts of the judo uniform and describe how they are worn.
6. Give the reasoning behind regular washing of the judo gi.

True-False Questions

1. Dojo, translated literally, means "gymnasium."
2. *Tatami* are vinyl-covered straw mats for judo.
3. The judo gi is made up of jacket, pants and belt.
4. The sleeves of the jacket should fall between the wrist and the halfway mark of the lower forearm.
5. Judo gi need not be washed regularly.
6. The granny knot is commonly used to tie the belt.

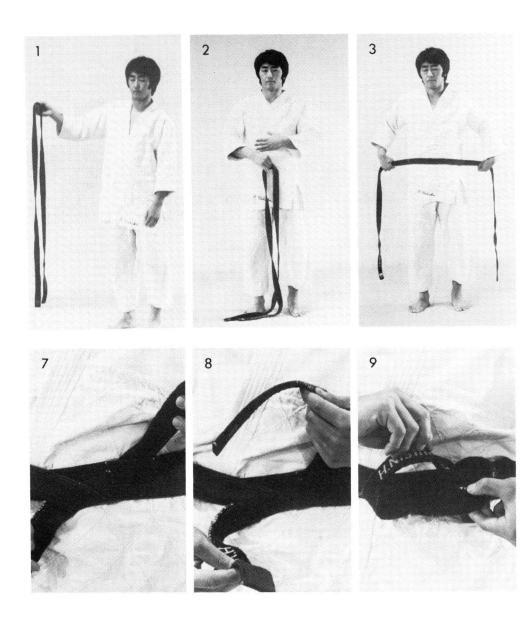

TYING THE BELT

(1) Hold the belt at its center so that both ends are even. (2) Place the left lapel of your judo gi over the right and press the belt's center against your abdomen. (3) Keep the belt's center against the gi and bring both ends out to your sides. (4) Now wrap the belt back around your waist, crossing one side over the other as they come behind you. (5) Then, bring the ends forward and around your waist a second time. (6) Take the end in your right hand and flap it over the end in your left. Then, slide it under both layers of belting,

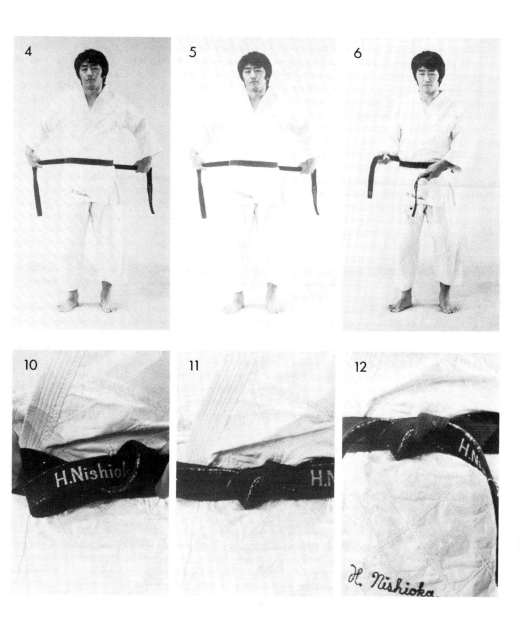

pulling it over and out. (7-9) Fasten the belt with a square knot: with the uppermost end, form a downward loop, the belt tail pointing to your right. Take the other end and slip it to the left through the loop. (10) Pull the knot tight. (11) Let both ends hang. Your belt is now tied correctly. (12) If tied incorrectly, the ends of your belt will not fall nicely to either side of the knot but will hang one above and one below, in a granny knot.

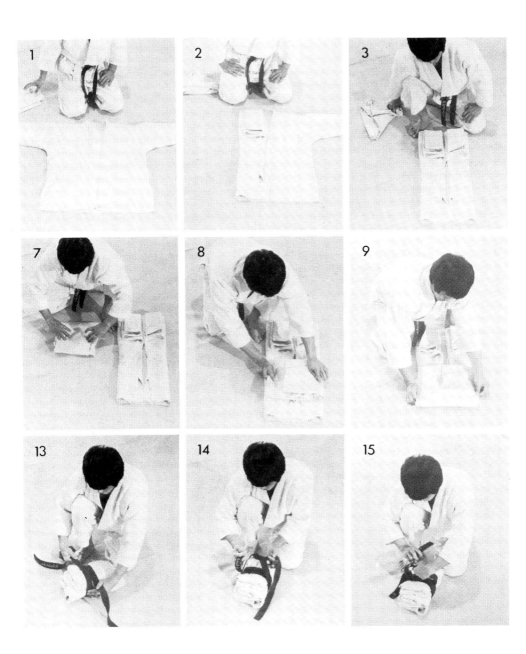

FOLDING THE JUDO GI

(1) Lay the judo gi out flat. (2&3) Fold the side seams in toward the center. Then fold the sleeves back and forth three times, accordion style. At this point, leave a slight gap between both halves to facilitate easy folding. (4) Lay the pants out flat. (5) Fold them in half, lengthwise. (6&7) Then, folding it in thirds, place the drawstring section beneath the lower pant legs. (8) Now

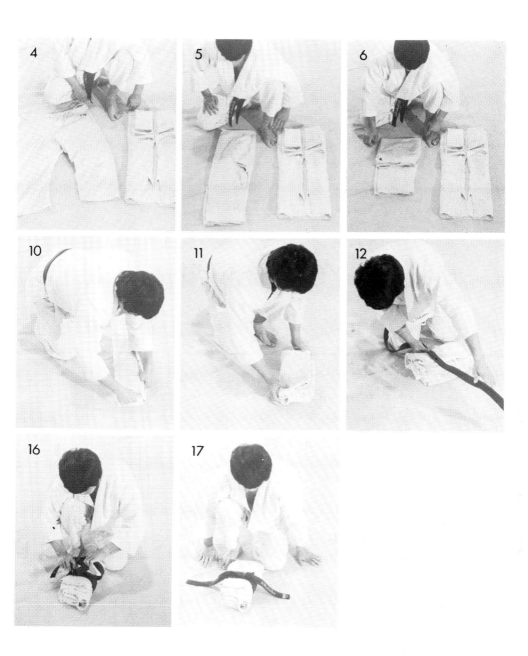

place the pants on the judo gi, positioning them roughly four to six inches from the gi's bottom edge. (9) Flap the bottom edge of the gi snugly over the pants. (10) Then fold the gi in half lengthwise. (11) Fold it in half crosswise. (12-17) Take the belt and, using a square knot, tie it crosswise around the gi as shown in the section on tying the belt.

Chapter III

TECHNIQUES OF JUDO

PREPARATION TO LEARNING JUDO

The basic skills are divided into two categories: the preparation stage and the technique stage.

The preparation stage is divided into methods of salutation, grips, methods of moving and falling techniques.

The main reason for the salutation (bowing to competitors and officials) is to show one's respect and gratitude. This respect and gratitude are accorded to the *sensei* or instructor for imparting his knowledge to the student, to the dojo or practice hall without which one would not be able to learn judo, and to the practice partner without whose presence the practitioner would not be able to develop techniques and progress.

The bow is executed at the following times:

1. When entering and leaving the dojo or practice hall.
2. When getting on or off the mat area.
3. Before and after practice sessions.
4. Before and after practicing with an opponent.
5. Before and after a match.
6. Before and after receiving an award.

It should be noted here that bowing before and after a match is a somewhat different situation in that instead of showing respect and gratitude, the bow is here meant to signify an acknowledgment of the state of competition; that is to say, the two contestants, whether they be classmates or the best of friends, are out to win. Therefore, from the time they bow at the beginning of the match to the end of the match when they again bow, they are not to consider themselves close friends. In other words, the time between the two bows should be considered a time for all-out fair play.

GRIPPING (KUMIKATA)

Judo, because of the type of activity it is, requires that practitioners hold onto each other to execute a technique. The strong judo uniform (judo gi) affords the practitioner many places to grip his opponent. Although the styles of gripping (kumikata) vary from practitioner to practitioner, there is a standard, accepted manner of gripping the opponent's uniform.

When gripping the opponent according to standard methods, the right hand grips the opponent's left lapel while the left hand grips the opponent's right sleeve. Normally, in this gripping position, both persons have their right feet extended one step forward.

If the person is left-handed and feels more comfortable in a left stance, then he should be doing the opposite of his right-handed partner; that is to say, his left hand should be on his opponent's right lapel while his right hand needs to be on the opponent's left sleeve.

There are numerous ways in which to hold onto your opponent. Nonetheless, here only two basic hand positions will be covered: the right-hand grip and the left-hand grip. The right-hand grip is usually used by right-handed persons applying a right-sided technique. A left-hand grip is usually used by a left-hander using a left-sided technique. A right-hander will hold the opponent's left lapel and right sleeve. The left-handed person will do the opposite.

MOVING

Moving one's feet or walking in judo is important, as the practitioner must learn to move with economy and purpose. When in motion, the practitioner must shift his weight about so as to leave no openings for an opponent to come in and attack. At the same time, he must move about, looking for an opportunity to attack

1

REI (SALUTATION)

RITSU REI
(STANDING BOW)

(1) Stand erect with your feet together. Place your open hands slightly forward along your thighs.
(2) Bend forward slightly at the
waist. As you do so, let your hands
glide down your legs.

2

ZA REI
(SEATED BOW)

(1) Sit comfortably with your knees together, feet tucked under your buttocks. Place your open hands over your upper thighs. (2) Bend forward at the hips, remembering to keep them low. As you do so, let your hands, facing inward at 45-degree angles, slide over your thighs to the mat.

his opponent and throw him. This constant shifting of position in judo is done to precipitate mistakes and increase the number of opportunities to attack. It is usually during the process of shuffling that techniques are applied. This is because the other person is trying to regain his equilibrium and is anatomically off balance.

In an effort to move about with economy of purpose, the practitioner must follow certain guiding rules:

1. As much as possible, keep most of your bodyweight evenly distributed over your base of support and line of gravity.

2. Avoid crossing your feet when moving about.

3. Avoid bringing your feet together when moving.

4. Avoid rhythmical, bouncing-type moves.

5. When moving, shuffle your feet slightly above the mat in short steps and move in lateral, oblique and circular motions as much as possible.

6. Keep your knees slightly flexed or bent while on the move.

7. If your opponent is bigger than you, try to move him more. If he is smaller than you, try not to move as much.

FALLING TECHNIQUES

In order for the beginning student to progress safely in judo, he must first master the techniques of falling. Any student who does not have a firm foundation in falling techniques will not progress because of his fear of being thrown and his inability to land on the mat without being hurt. If the practitioner is afraid of being thrown, he will concentrate on possible injuries rather than on trying to overcome his opponent. Mastering techniques of falling will diminish the fear of being thrown and instill confidence in the possibility of throwing the opponent.

There are four basic directions in which falls can be directed. Thus, there are four types of falls intrinsic to the practice of judo: the front fall, back fall, side fall and the rolling fall.

THE RIGHT NATURAL GRIP

The right natural grip is the most common grip in judo. To execute it, use your left hand and grip your opponent's right sleeve just under the elbow. With your right hand, hold his left lapel firmly. The right feet of both persons are usually placed forward slightly. Hold your body relatively erect.

THE LEFT NATURAL GRIP

In applying the left natural grip, take hold of your opponent's left sleeve by placing your right hand just behind his elbow. With your left hand, hold firmly to his right lapel. You may want to place your left foot slightly forward.

THE JUDO SHUFFLE

To shuffle to your left, (1) assume the *shizentai* (natural posture) position. (2&3) Move your left foot to the side and shift your weight to it. Remember that this movement should be more a shuffle than a high step. (4) With the toes pointing outward and dragging on the mat, bring your right foot toward your left until it is no less than six inches away from your left. (5&6) Shifting your weight to your right foot, begin moving your left into the next step. To shuffle to the right, lead with your right foot, letting your left trail after it.

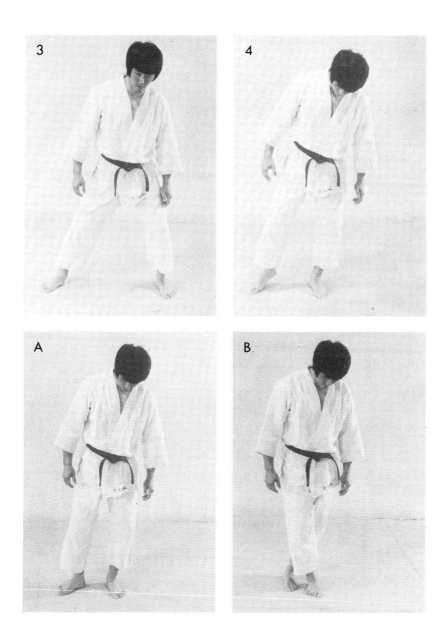

Remember that most judo movements are executed in random directions and depend on the push and pull of the two participants. Therefore, become proficient in shuffling at all angles and in all directions. (A) A no-no in judo movement is bringing your feet together too closely. (B) Another taboo is cross-stepping. Both (A&B) narrow your base of support and decrease your stability, thereby leaving you vulnerable to various throws and making it easier for your opponent to throw you off balance.

BACK FALLS SEATED AND STANDING

SEATED

From a seated position, roll back and let your feet ride up. Slap the mat as the small of your back hits the mat. Let the momentum carry your buttocks up.

Common Errors

1. Hands are too far away from the body. They should be no more than six inches to a foot away from the side of your body.

2. Head is not tucked in, chin to chest. Common cause of concussion.

3. The buttocks are not raised after the slap.

STANDING

In the *standing back fall*, the only thing to remember is to squat straight down before rolling back to slap.

SIDE FALLS LYING DOWN AND STANDING

LYING DOWN

Move from side-to-side. When moving to the right, slap with the palm of the right hand. When moving to the left, slap with the palm of the left hand. The hand not in use should be placed on the stomach.

Keep the head up off the mat, the legs slightly bent and apart; slap six inches to a foot away from the body.

UKEMI
(back falls)

(1&2) From a standing position, squat straight down, placing the hands in front, arms slightly bent. (3) Roll back, touching the buttocks to the mat. (4) Continue to roll back, bringing arms down in a whiplike motion; palms down, about six inches away from the body. (5) Once the slap is complete, let the leg naturally roll back and over the head. (6&7) When the legs have reached their peak and begin to swing in the opposite direction, use your momentum to bring the body up again to a standing position. This action may be repeated several times. Some schools may use the seated backfall only, in which case merely repeat steps pictured (3-6).

UKEMI (side fall [from standing])

(1) Stand with the feet apart at shoulder-width. (2) Kick the left foot across to the right side and raise the left hand to the right side. (3) Squat straight down, continuing to raise the left arm. (4) Continue to descend until the left buttock hits the floor. (5) Now roll back and begin to bring the arm down to

UKEMI (side fall [on mat])

(1) Lying on one side, the legs are apart, the head off the mat, left hand on the stomach, the right hand palm down on the mat about six to 10 inches away from the bent knee, the judoka is ready for the side-fall exercise. (2) Rolling to the left side, the legs are raised high, the right hand goes to the stomach as the left hand descends to the mat in a whip-like motion to the opposite side. (3) Impact is made about six to 10 inches away from the bent left knee, palm down. (4) Once finished, the body and arms are ready for the return once again to the right side.

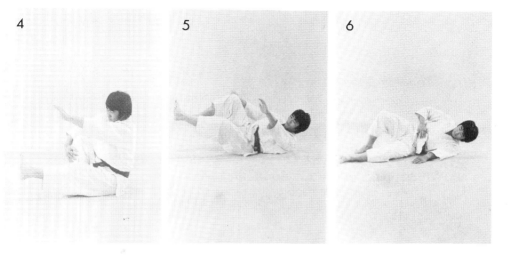

the mat forcefully. (6) The side of the left leg should make contact with the mat at about the same time as the left hand slaps the mat. The right hand goes to the stomach. This side fall is usually repeated several times by getting up and alternating sides.

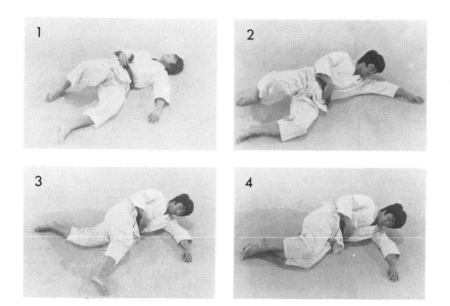

FOUR COMMON ERRORS IN THE SIDE FALL

(1) The most common mistake made by a beginner is resting the head on the mat while attempting to execute a proper side fall. (2) Reaching too high with the slapping arm is another frequent error, which reduces the capacity to absorb shock. (3) Another shortcoming, the knees are brought together when turning from side to side. (4) Reaching over of the leg opposite to the hand that does the slapping is another failing. This action throws the body out of alignment and often causes the person to roll too much.

Common Errors

1. Slapping with the left hand when rolling to the right and vice versa.

2. Keeping the knees together or crossed.

3. Slapping with the wrong side of the hand. The slap is with the palm side to the mat.

4. Slapping too far away from the body.

5. Not keeping the head off the mat with the chin tucked in.

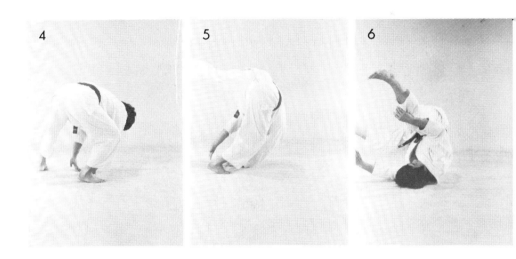

ZEMPOKAITEN UKEMI (rolling falls)

(1) Stand erect with feet a shoulder's-width apart. (2) Step forward with the right foot naturally turned outward to the left. (3) Bend at the knees and hips and place the hands between the right and left feet, fingers pointed towards each other. (4) Now lean forward so that the toes of the right foot are your only means of support. (5) Now look back at the left foot, let go and begin to roll over. The judoka in this position is rolling over his right shoulder with the head tucked in. (6) Once contact is made, continue through, getting ready to bring the right hand to the mat and the left to the stomach. (7) Continuing through, the body should roll to the right side and (8) end up in the same position as in the side falls. This ukemi is often repeated to the opposite side and is often alternated as one traverses the mat area. (9) A common error consists of not pointing the fingers inward, a mistake which may cause injury to the wrist.

STANDING FALLS

For the most part, standing falls are the same except that after the slap one rolls to a standing position. When rolling down, squat straight down before rolling back to slap.

STANDING ROLLING FALLS

1. Assume a stance with feet a shoulderwidth apart.
2. Take a step forward without narrowing the overall width of the stance.

3. Place hand on the mat halfway between right and left legs.

4. Bend the knees slightly.

5. Make sure that the fingers are pointing in towards each other.

6. Now lean forward until the right toe is barely keeping your body from rolling over.

7. Next, let go and roll over, slapping as you would in a side-fall position.

8. Now try from the opposite side.

Common Errors

1. Rolling to the side of the body instead of over the head and shoulder.

2. Rolling directly overhead as in a somersault.

The technique stage of judo consists of standing or throwing techniques and mat or grappling techniques.

THROWING

The classic book, *The Canon of Judo*, by Kyuzu Mifune, lists some 95 throwing variations. *Dynamic Judo* by Kudo Kazuzo lists 52 standing techniques. *The Sport of Judo* by Kobayashi and Sharp contains 28 throws. While many of the throws provided in these books are excellent, it is perhaps improbable that a beginner could learn so many variations of throws. In modern sport judo, there are only about 10 techniques which are consistently used to gain the advantage over an opponent.

Most major judo competitors, after gaining a basic knowledge of the techniques available, will select a favorite and perfect it by constant application. Some competitors will have a back-up technique as well, in case the first technique is unsuccessful. Still others will use a combination of two or three techniques.

For the most part, a fair grasp of judo may be had by learning 10 to 15 throws. Those wishing more knowledge of other throws may study further in the books previously suggested. *Vital Judo*, a current best-seller by Isao Okano, shows many unorthodox techniques executed by top-level Japanese competitors.

This book contains 15 throws which include most of the 10

most popular techniques in competition judo. The other five techniques have been added to aid the judoka in developing an aesthetic awareness of movement and spatial relationships.

The techniques have been selected so that each of the six categories of throws is touched upon. The categories are: Te-waza (hand techniques), koshi-waza (hip techniques), ashi-waza (foot techniques), masu-setemi-waza (back sacrifice techniques), yoke-sutemi-waza (side sacrifice techniques), kaeshi-waza (countertechniques).

Ideally, it is nice to have knowledge of all 40 throws and be able to execute them with expert proficiency; however, this would usually take a number of years to realize. These 40 throws are commonly referred to as the *gokyo no waza.*

The modern American judoka need know only 15 throws to begin with. The following maneuvers were selected on the basis of the popularity of the throws in tournament play as well as their ability to stimulate the flowing feeling which the technique suggests.

The sequence of the throws is arranged in a lesson-plan order so that the beginning student can advance in a cycle of throws, beginning with foot technique, a hip technique and a hand technique—then, returning, to advance by sequences of foot, hip and hand throws, etcetera. The last three are sacrifice techniques (and one countermove). The order of the throws is as follows:

1. **Osoto-gari** *(outside major reap)*
2. **Ogoshi** *(hip throw)*
3. **Morote Seoinage** *(two-arm shoulder throw)*
4. **Okuri-ashi-barai** *(chasing foot sweep)*
5. **Harai goshi** *(hip sweep)*
6. **Ippon Seoinage** *(one-arm shoulder throw)*
7. **Ouchi-gari** *(inside major reap)*
8. **Tsuri-komigoshi** *(hanging hip throw)*
9. **Tai-otoshi** *(body drop)*
10. **Kouchi-gari** *(inside minor reap)*
11. **Uchimata** *(inner thigh throw)*
12. **Soto-makikomi** *(wrap-around throw)*
13. **Yoko-guruma** *(side wheel)*
14. **Tomoe-nage** *(stomach throw)*
15. **Ushiro-goshi** *(reverse hip)*

OSOTO-GARI

Many tall champions of the past have taken advantage of their long-legged reach by applying *osoto-gari*. First All-Japan Champion Yasuici Matsumoto, 1965 All-Japan Champion Seiji Sakaguchi and, more recently, Isamu Sonoda, the World Champion, have made successful use of this throw.

To execute it, step forward with the left foot to the side of the opponent. The upper body is pulled in tight so that the right sides of the bodies are contiguous. The knee should be slightly bent,

and the weight of the thrower should be on the balls of the feet. Now the right foot shoots through with the toe pointed. The foot is extended to the point where one can pick up speed on the return swing. Hooking up, the right foot follows through without touching the mat, thus avoiding any loss of momentum. The left hand should pull downward while the right arm drives across, over the shoulder and downward.

OSOTO-GARI
(outside major reap)

(1) Assume the right grip. (2) Next, step forward with the left foot, placing it far enough away from the opponent to leave an opening for following with the right leg. Here both arms of the opponent should pull him forward while the thrower moves closer and faster by stepping into the opponent. (3) The right leg follows through, the toe pointed, the leg outstretched ready for the backward reap. (4) The reap is forceful as the back of the knees meet. (5) The right arm pushes forward as the left arm pulls downward. (6) The follow-through finds the foot raised high, toe pointed.

OGOSHI

Ogoshi is often referred to as the father of hip throws, since the stepping position serves as the basis for many other hip throws, the basic foot step being that of an "X-in-the-box step." (Page 46-47)

This throw is a must for the beginning student.

The first step is placed in front of the opponent's right foot while the right hand prepares to encircle the waist. Most of the weight should be on the ball of the right foot to facilitate the pivoting of the first foot when the second foot enters. When the second foot is in place, the X is completed. At this point, the knees should be bent to lower the center of gravity, and the upper body ought to be leaning forward. The right hand can grasp the belt behind the opponent or can be placed on his back. The left hand should pull forward and across the chest.

Simultaneously, begin to pull the opponent up and over by extending the knees and turning counterclockwise. Once he's in the air, guide him down and hold onto his right sleeve.

Courtine and Pariset, two great French champions of the 1950s

45

OGOSHI
(hip throw)

(1&2) From the right natural position, the thrower releases the lapel and steps forward with the right foot. (3) The thrower's right hand reaches around the opponent's waist and at the same time brings the left leg back. The knees are bent, the left tautly pulling forward, the hip bent to the side and the upper torso leaning to the front. (4-6) Once in position, the head is lowered, the upper torso torquing to the left while pulling with the left arm, the knees extended for the lift. The right arm assists in the pull, and it's up and over.

2

3

5

6

MOROTE SEOINAGE

The two-arm *seoinage* is a favorite with the small man. It has been used successfully by Eiji Maruki, 1967 World Champion, and by Isao Okano, World Champion 1965, Olympic Gold Medalist and three-time All-Japan Champion. Many of Okano's opponents claim that his entry is so fast that one only realizes he has been thrown after the second bounce.

The stepping on the *morote seoinage* is similar to that of the *ogoshi*. The feet follow the same X pattern and the knees are bent. In contrast to the hip throw, however, the right natural grip is

maintained. On the first step across, the elbow is bent and prepared to enter under the opponent's right armpit. The hips are
placed against the opponent's right thigh. The right hand is curled
forward while still gripping. The elbow should be held fairly close
to the body in an acute angle.

Once in place, quickly pull forward with both hands and
straighten the ankle and knees. When your opponent is in the air,
you should guide him down by holding onto his right sleeve.

MOROTE-SEOI-NAGE
(two-arm shoulder throw)

(1) Contemplating the entry from a right natural grip, the attacker readies to pull the opponent to the side. (2) Now the attacker steps forward with the right foot, the right elbow bending and the left arm pulling the opponent to the side. (3) The left leg is brought around and placed in position slightly deeper than it was in the first step. Note here the attacker's right foot has pivoted to allow more counterclockwise motion. The knees are bent, as is the hip. The attacker is leaning forward, pulling the opponent down into his bent arm with both arms. (4) Continuing the throw, the knees are extended, causing the opponent to come up off the mat. (5) The arms and torso do the rest: the arms pull as the torso torques to the left. (6) Once the opponent is sufficiently over the thrower's right arm, he releases and holds the opponent up for support.

OKURI-ASHI-BARAI

In 1960, 1964 and 1965, Anton Geesink used this technique to fight his way to the top. The first non-Japanese to win the World Championship (1960), he won an Olympic Gold Medal in 1964 and defended his title successfully in 1965.

The *okuri-ashi-barai* is a rhythm technique that exploits the movement of the opponent's feet.

Move the opponent to his right by taking a large step in that direction. As the opponent's left leg endeavors to catch up, begin the sweep by forcefully sweeping the sole of your foot to the

Anton Geesink (Netherlands) sweeps Akio Kaminaga (Japan), '64 Olympics

opponent's left instep. The object is to add impetus to an already moving foot. When you are sweeping it, the opponent's left foot should be pushed into his right foot. The left hand is pushed upward as the right hand is pulled downward. Most experts, when sweeping, will thrust the stomach forward for added reach, being careful to keep the chin pulled in.

After the opponent is airborne, release the left hand, but hold onto the right lapel to guide the opponent down.

OKURI-ASHI-BARAI
(sending foot sweep)

(1) Preparing for the *okuri-ashi-barai*, the right natural grip is assumed. (2) The thrower, moving laterally, takes a large step, hoping to draw his opponent out in the same direction. (3) As the opponent takes the side step and begins to bring his feet together, the thrower begins his sweep from behind, adding to the momentum of the opponent's feet coming together. (4) The right hand is brought downward and the left hand is raised. The knee is straight, the hip thrust forward, the chin tucked in and the foot sweeps hard against the opponent's instep. (5&6) After the opponent is in the air, the knee may be bent as well as the hips, but not until the peak of the throw has been passed.

HARAI-GOSHI

Legend has it that the *harai-goshi* was originally devised by Dr. Kano to counteract an opponent's hop-around move to avoid ogoshi. When the opponent stepped around the ogoshi, Dr. Kano merely placed his right leg out and tripped him in midair.

Since then, the ogoshi has evolved into a technique used by many big men. Among the users of harai goshi have been Akio Kaminaga, twice All-Japan Champion, and Wilhelm Ruska of Holland, twice World Champion.

In entering harai-goshi, the triangle formation is used. The first step is to the top of the triangle.

The second foot is placed near the base as the arms are bent to pull the opponent in close. The right hip is placed against the lower abdomen of the opponent. In the next instant, the right leg is swept backwards without touching the ground. Notice the toe is pointed, the body leans forward, and there is a torquing action, counterclockwise. Once the opponent is in the air, the sweeping foot may be brought down for balance. Again the opponent is braced.

Ueno throws Nakatani

HARAI-GOSHI
(hip sweep)

(1&2) From the right natural grip the thrower steps forward with the right foot pointed laterally inward. (3) Next, the opponent is drawn in with both arms while stepping around with the left foot. Here the hip does not enter as deeply as in the *ogoshi* but is about three-quarters of the way in. (4) Simultaneously, the arms continue the pull to the front, while the right leg, with the toes pointed, reaps back against the opponent's right leg. (5&6) Then with a final pull-over, the *harai-goshi* is complete.

IPPON SEOINAGE

Many a championship has been won with the *ippon seoinage*. On the list of famous users are Isao Inokuma, twice All-Japan Champion; World Champion and Olympic Gold Medalist Isao Okano; Doug Nelson, United States Grand Champion and Olympian—and, of course, the famous Kimura Masahiko, the undefeated champion of Japan.

This technique offers an advantage in that the aggressor need only hold on with one hand, leaving the other free to avoid an opponent's grip.

To enter, the right foot is placed in front of the opponent's right foot. The right arm is in position to instantly go under the opponent's armpit. As the right arm ascends to the armpit, the left hand pulls the opponent forward so that the opponent's armpit rests on the biceps. At the same time, the left leg should shift into position. Notice here that the knees are bent and the hip is placed against the opponent's right leg. His right arm is pinned against the chest, with his body leaning forward. Once in, the knees are straightened, lifting the opponent off the ground. The body is torqued counterclockwise, and the opponent is over. The right arm in this throw imitates the circular motion of an ocean wave breaking.

Isao Okano sends Sato skyward, All-Japan Championships

IPPON-SEOI-NAGE
(one-arm shoulder throw)

(1&2) From the right natural position, the thrower releases his right arm and drops it as he begins to step in with the right foot. (3) Simultaneously, the opponent's armpit is drawn down to the biceps by the thrower's downward, left-handed pull; then the hip is swung into place by bringing the left leg back. Note the upraised hand of the thrower. (4) Now in place, the knees are extended as the opponent is pulled onto the thrower's back. (5) Continuing the motion, the upper torso and head rotate to the left as the opponent goes over. (6) Lastly, the opponent is seen being held by the thrower at the finish of the throw.

OUCHI-GARI

The *ouchi-gari* is generally used as a setup for a combination technique set, such as ouchi to taiotoshi or ouchi to ippon seoinage. However, it has been used effectively as a technique and has its own merits as a point-getter.

Among the users of the ouchi are Hisashi Tsuzawa, middleweight World Champion; Paul Maruyama, 154-pound United States Champion and Olympian; Irwin Cohen, 176-pound United States Grand Champion 1974, and Olympian.

Using the triangle form, the first step is the top of the triangle with the right foot. The second foot is brought in close to the first foot, but not too close. You want to be able to push to the opponent's rear. The hands are pulled in.

Cut to the rear in a circular motion, pivoting on the left foot and keeping the right foot pointed. The arms push the opponent to the rear.

OUCHIGARI
(inside major reap)

(1) From the right natural position, the thrower steps forward with the right foot. (2) Second, the left arm of the thrower pulls and lifts the arm of the opponent as the left leg is drawn up behind the right foot. (3) Proceeding, the right leg now travels in a small clockwise, circular pattern with the toes pointed. It catches at the back of the opponent's knee. (4&5) The thrower pushes with the right arm, pulls with the left, kicks back with the right leg and pushes into the opponent with the left leg. (6) The thrower may allow his momentum to pull him down, or he may wish to catch his balance by dropping his sweeping leg down.

SODE TSURIKOMI GOSHI

In recent times, the *sode tsurikomi* was brought into play by a competitor named Iwata. He defeated several heavyweight competitors who outweighed him by as much as 90 pounds. The power of the throw so impressed many bigger competitors that they also began to use it. Among them, Jim Wooley of the United States placed fourth in the Olympic Games in Munich.

To execute the *sode tsurikomi goshi*, the right hand must first be inverted so that the thumb is on the inside and is pointing towards you. Assume this grip right from the beginning.

Now use the X in the box step. As the right foot shoots across, the opponent's left hand is raised high. As the second foot turns in, the knees are bent and the opponent's body is pulled forward flush against the right side. To throw, the knees are extended and the body torqued. Notice that the right arm pulls the opponent over in a high arc, while the elbow is kept against the opponent's arm. The throw is completed with the bracing of the opponent's arm.

Shinohara

SODE-TSURIKOMI-GOSHI
(suspending sleeve hip throw)

(1&2) From a right natural grip, the thrower's right hand shifts from lapel to a position gripping the sleeve, with the right palm facing upwards. As the thrower enters, he raises the opponent's right arm high in the air. (3) As the left foot is brought back, the hip is thrown across; the right arm is still high, the left arm pulls the opponent's right arm in tight and the knees are bent. (4&5) Finally, the opponent is hoisted off his feet as the thrower extends his knees. The upraised arm begins to pull the opponent over.

2

3

5

71

TAI OTOSHI

The *tai otoshi* was one of Isao Inokuma's favorite throws. Once, Mr. Inokuma whipped an opponent over so hard with the tai otoshi that he rendered him unconscious. Its power comes from the snapping action of the leg, combined with the pulling down of the arms.

To execute the tai otoshi, step across with the right foot while pulling the opponent to his right side so that most of his weight is on his right foot. Quickly bring your left foot around and place it in front of the opponent's left foot.

Next, step across with your right leg and block his knee with your bent knee. Make sure that your right foot balances on the ball of the foot so the nap of your knee is flush against the opponent's shin. To do this, a low stance must be assumed.

The hand continues to pull the opponent forward until his weight is on the right foot. Sometimes the palm of the right hand is placed against the opponent's chin to push him off balance.

To snap over, merely straighten the right leg and pull the opponent forward and downward.

jor Maruyama vs. Masterson in U.S. Nationals

TAI-OTOSHI
(body drop)

(1) From the right grip position, the thrower readies for the *tai-otoshi*. (2) Stepping forward, the thrower leads the opponent to the left, causing him to adjust his balance slightly. (3) The left foot is now swung around and placed in front of the opponent's left foot. At this point, the body of the thrower is essentially facing the same direction as the opponent. The thrower's right arm is against the chest, and the hand on the judo gi is near the opponent's chin. (4&5) The thrower drops suddenly, bending both knees. It is crucial here that the right knee be flush against the opponent's leg. The thrower should be on the ball of his foot. The opponent's body position should be such that the weight is on his right foot. (6) With a quick extension of the thrower's knee, the opponent should snap up in the air. (7) The hands should be used also; right hand pushes, left hand pulls until the tai-otoshi is complete.

KOUSHI GARI

Virtually every major competitor makes use of the *kouchi gari.* The main advantage of this throw is that it can easily be applied without too much risk of a countermove or of leaving an opening for the opponent. It is also useful as a setup for a combination of techniques (kouchi to ouchi gari, uchimata to kouchi, etcetera).

The kouchi, like the ouchi gari, is used on opponents with a tendency to sit on their heels.

To begin, step to the top of the triangle, a little to the left side. Immediately bring your left foot behind the heel of your opponent's right foot. Then extend the right foot, placing it between the opponent's legs, cutting forward with the sole of the foot against the opponent's Achilles tendon or heel. The reap should be executed in the same direction pointed to by the toes of the opponent.

The left hand throughout the throw should be pulled downward. The right hand, once foot contact is made, should be driven over the opponent's shoulder and downwards.

ames Bregman in the Olympics, 1964

KOUCHI-GARI
(inside major reap)

(1) The attacker assumes a right natural grip. (2) With a quick tug of the arms, the thrower steps forward with the right foot. The tug causes the opponent to react by leaning to the rear slightly. (3) The thrower draws his left foot up behind the his right until he is sideways to his opponent. (4) Quickly, the right leg is extended to place the reaping foot behind the opponent's right foot. (5) Continuing the motion, the opponent's right foot is reaped forcefully in the direction of the pointing toes. Here the right arm should be pushing to the rear while the left pulls in a downward direction. (6&7) Once the opponent begins to descend, the thrower may bend his leg.

UCHIMATA

Next to the seoinage, the *uchimata* is probably the most colorful and popular technique in competition judo. Countless champions have used the uchimata in a myriad of ways.

Here in the United States, the most famous of the uchimata kings have been Tosh Seino, United States Champion, Pan-American and Air Force Champion; James Bregman, Bronze Medalist in the 1964 Olympic Games, and more recently, Pat Burris, Olympian and United States Lightweight Champion.

Use the triangle step. First the right foot is placed at the top of the triangle slightly to the left side and pointing to the left.

The left foot swings around and goes to the base of the triangle. Simultaneously, the arms pull the opponent forward and flush. Note here that the knees are slightly bent. Next, the right leg shoots back, right toe pointed, body leaning forward. The head is lowered, the right leg raised high in the air, and the body is torqued to the left. As the opponent comes down, hold onto the sleeve to brace his fall.

Seino taking R. Shibata for a high ride

UCHIMATA
(inner thigh throw)

(1) Thinking of the *uchimata*, the thrower readies himself. (2) Now the right foot steps forward and in front of the opponent. (3) Pull the opponent in close with both arms while stepping into place with the left foot. Note here the left foot is in deeper than the right. The knee is bent. (4) Continuing the pull, the thrower's right leg sweeps back between the opponent's legs with the toes pointed. (5) The head is now lowered and the right leg raised high in the air. (6) The thrower's upper torso and head torque to the left side, and the opponent goes over.

SOTOMAKIKOMI

In 1967, Mitsuo Matsunaga became World Champion. One of the throws he used to get to the top was the *sotomakikomi*.

The sotomakikomi uses "the X in the box step." Your right foot is placed in front of the opponent's right foot. In the same motion, the left arm pulls forward while the right arm is released from the lapel and is brought over the opponent's head. The second foot is brought back, the body turned and the arm pulled in tightly. Continuing through, the right leg steps across the opponent's leg, blocking his escape. Following through, the body is turned to the left.

Geesink (Holland) vs. Sone (Japan)

SOTO-MAKIKOMI
(outside wraparound throw)

(1&2) When entering the *soto-maki-komi*, the right foot steps forward, the right hand is raised and sweeps across, as the left hand begins to pull. (3) As the left leg is brought back, the left arm pulls, aided by the torque of the upper torso. (4) Now the right leg drives across, locking the opponent's knees. (5) The body begins to lean forward as the right hand starts to descend. (6&7) Locked in place, the right foot drives off the mat as the thrower begins to do a rolling fall. Once airborne, the thrower continues his momentum, pulling the opponent over the top and finishing the throw.

YOKO GURUMA

This technique, though not used too often in tournament play, is essential to master in order to practice countering an opponent's move in a smooth, flowing fashion. "Using your opponent's force in order to throw him"—the essence of judo—is imparted by the feeling of this throw.

As the opponent enters, lower your center of gravity and stop

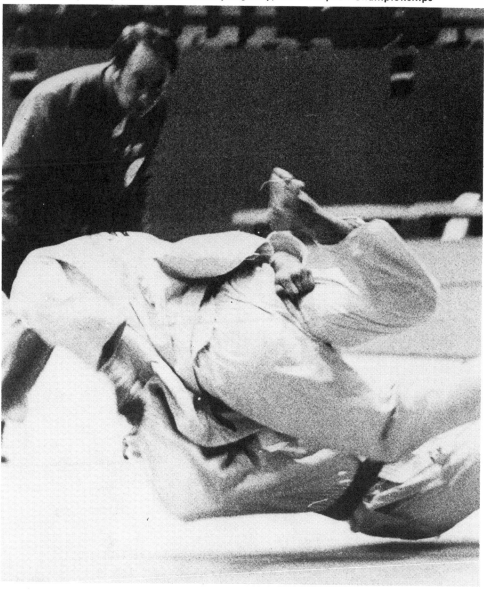

his attempted throw by grabbing him around the waist. Bring your right foot over the opponent's right leg, then shoot it through by turning to face him. At this juncture, he will be pulling down, and you will be deliberately going to your back. Try to strike the mat with your left side. As you descend, pull the opponent over you and throw him to his back.

YOKO-GURUMA
(side wheel)

(1&2) The attacker enters into a hip technique while the defender shifts slightly to the right, lowers his center of gravity and encircles the opponent's torso. (3) Quickly, the defender places his right leg between his opponent's legs. (4) As defender's leg continues through, his upper body should begin to torque, pulling the opponent with both arms. Here the body's gravitational pull will aid in bringing the opponent down. Notice that the right knee has gone through and ends in a bent knee position, with the sole of the foot on the mat. The left leg is in front of the opponent's leg as he goes over. (5) In the final position, the counterattacker should be on his left side, looking over his left shoulder at his thrown opponent.

TOMOE-NAGE

Five-times United States Champion Sumikichi Nozaki employed *tomoe-nage* with frequent success. Although it is not extremely popular in tournament play, it is used often in randori practice by those practitioners confident of being able to exploit the failure of an opponent's attack.

Step forward on the left foot and place it between the opponent's legs. Quickly bring the right leg up and position it in the

opponent's stomach and begin a descent as though you were to sit in a chair that wasn't there. Keep the knees bent.

As the buttocks hit the mat, continue to pull him until his weight balances on your right foot. Extend your leg and pull him over. The left leg should be bent and lending support to your throw.

TOMOE-NAGE
(stomach throw)

(1) Assume a right natural grip and push slightly forward with the hands. (2) When the opponent reacts and pushes back, simultaneously step forward and between his legs with the left foot. (3) Immediately bring the right knee up. This will necessitate bending the knee and will also cause the attacker to lose his balance to the rear. (4) Using the backward, off-balance momentum, place the right foot against the opponent's stomach with the knee still bent. (5) As the opponent is pulled off balance, and his weight is felt on the right foot, begin to extend the right leg while continuing to pull with the arms. (6) Notice also that the left leg is continuously bent. This gives the thrower more stabilization and control. The tomoe-nage is now complete.

95

USHIRO GOSHI

Another of Mitsuo Matsunaga's favorite throws, the *ushiro goshi* can be used effectively by any judoka.

Anticipating the opponent's entry, the hips should be lowered, arms grasping around the opponent's waist. Once set, lift your opponent up by arching backwards. The momentum should raise the opponent's legs. Once they have reached their peak, pike at the hips and pull the opponent downwards and onto his back.

ergei Suslin finds another victim

USHIRO-GOSHI
(reverse hip)

(1) From the right natural grip, the attacker begins to enter with a hip technique. Here the important point is for the defender to attune himself to anticipate the entry. (2) As the attacker enters, the defender must lower his center of gravity by bending at the knees and encircling the opponent's body with both hands. The hip of the defender should be below and slightly underneath the entry. (3) This position will allow the defender to extend and lift the opponent by extending the knees. Thrust the hips upwards and forwards. (4&5) Once the opponent has reached maximum height, the defender bends at the hips and brings the opponent down, completing the counterthrow or *ushiro-goshi*.

WHAT ARE THE GRAPPLING TECHNIQUES OF JUDO?

Grappling techniques fall into three categories, and the techniques can be troublesome if proper guidelines are not followed.

The three categories are *osaekomiwaza* (pinning techniques), *shimewaza* (choke techniques) and *kansetsuwaza* (arm techniques).

The pinning techniques render an opponent unable to move, while the person applying the pin has his legs relatively free to do as he pleases. For the beginner there are five fundamental pinning methods with which he should be familiar: *kesagatame, katagatame, yokoshihogatame, kamishihogatame, tateshihogatame*. These are discussed below.

Wilhelm Ruska (Holland) pins Kuzetsow (USSR), 1972 Olympics

KESA-GATAME

(1) In entering the *kesa-gatame*, the attacker must secure the opponent's right arm by gripping the judo gi just below the elbow with the left hand. (2) Now bring the right foot through, keeping the left foot bent for stability. Once through, the opponent's right arm should be held not only with the hand but with the arm pressing against the rib cage. The right arm should begin to encircle the neck of the opponent. (3) Next, lower the hips, spread the legs and pull the opponent's head up.

KESAGATAME

The right arm is placed about the neck. The left arm holds the opponent's arm in tightly. The legs are spread to give a wide base. The opponent's head is raised while applying pressure to his chest.

KATA-GATAME

(1) Kneeling beside the opponent, take your left hand and place it under the opponent's elbow. Now push the arm up and across the opponent's face. (2) Next bring the right arm around the opponent's neck. (3) Finally, clasp the hands together and squeeze both shoulders and arm as the right leg is passed through.

KATAGATAME

In the *katagatame*, the opponent's arm is pushed across his face. The arms encircle the opponent's arm and head. The leg may be placed, bent and flush, against the opponent's body.

Variation.

One may also sit out as in the kesagatame, the only difference here being that the opponent's arm is trapped.

KAMI-SHIHO-GATAME
(upper four-quarters hold)

(1) The attacker kneels at the head of the opponent to grip at the belt with both hands. (2) The belt is gripped, and the legs are spread and extended backwards. Here the attacker should force his hip downward, placing pressure on the opponent's head. Note that at this time the attacker is on his toes, allowing him quick mobility and enabling the attacker to place more downward pressure on the opponent's head.

KAMISHIHOGATAME

In the *kamishihogatame*, the arm goes over the opponent's arms. The belt is held, legs spread and hips are down.

YOKO-SHIHO-GATAME
(side four-quarters hold)

(1) Reach over the opponent's right shoulder and grip the judo gi along the spine. (2) Next, with the left hand, grip at the seam of the pants and pull up. (3) Finally, the hips should be lowered, the legs spread apart, with a general tightening up on the arms. Not pictured are the legs of the attacker, which may be extended, or one leg may be bent and brought in close to the opponent's ribs.

YOKOSHIHOGATAME

The right arm goes over the opponent's right shoulder and grips the back of the gi. The left arm goes under the crotch, slightly raising the opponent's buttocks off the mat.

TATE-SHIHO-GATAME
(face-to-face four-quarters hold)

(1) Kneeling beside the opponent, place your left hand beneath the elbow. (2) Straddle the opponent while pushing his arm across the face and encircling the neck with the right arm. (3) Now release the left hand and use the head to press the arm to the opponent's face. Once the left arm is free, grasp the encircling right hand to lock in his shoulder and head. The legs should encircle the opponent's legs and grapevine tightly.

TATESHIHOGATAME

As in the katagatame, the head and arm are encircled. In this technique, however, the aggressor rides over the opponent and grapevines both legs.

CHOKING

Choking methods are of two sorts. By applying pressure to the trachea of an opponent, you can cut off the oxygen supply to his lungs. The second method applies pressure to the carotid arteries, denying a blood supply to the brain. Of these, the latter technique is perhaps the more humane in that it is not as painful as applying pressure to the trachea. Use of these techniques is expressly limited to students over the age of 12.

JUJI-JIME
(cross choke)

(1) Place the right thumb on the inside of the opponent's right lapel. With the left hand, place the fingers to inside of the opponent's left lapel with the palm facing towards you. (2) Now simultaneously pull in and down with the left hand, while the right hand pulls in and the elbow goes across the opponent's neck for the choke.

OKURI-ERI-GIME
(assisting arm choke)

(1) From behind, using the right hand, grip the lapel. (2) With the left hand, come up under the chin and encircle the neck, gripping the lapel with the thumb to the inside of the judo gi. (3) Now pull in and down with the right arm and in and around with the left hand.

KATA-HA-JIME
(single-arm trap choke)

(1&2) From the regular *okuri-eri-gime* position, the attacker's right arm releases and is brought straight up. This will raise the opponent's arm and shoulder. The left hand remains gripping the judo gi under the chin. (3) Now

the right arm of the attacker is directed in the back of the opponent's head, trapping the arm high in the air. (4) Finally, the left arm pulls back and the right hand pushes forward.

HADAKA-JIME
(bare arm choke)

(1) Bring the right arm under and across the opponent's chin. (2) Now clasp the hands together with the right hand palm down. (3) Finally, push forward with the right shoulder and pull back with the clasped arms.

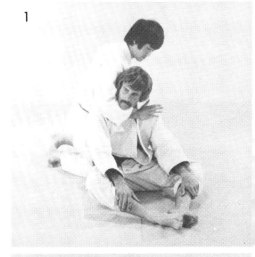

HADAKA-JIME VARIATION

(A&B) Reach around the opponent's neck with the right arm, palm down. (C) Now place the right hand on the biceps with the little finger at the bend of the elbow. (D&E) Next bend the left arm over the grasping right hand and place it behind the opponent's head. (F) Finally, squeeze in and backwards with the right arm while pushing forward with the right hand.

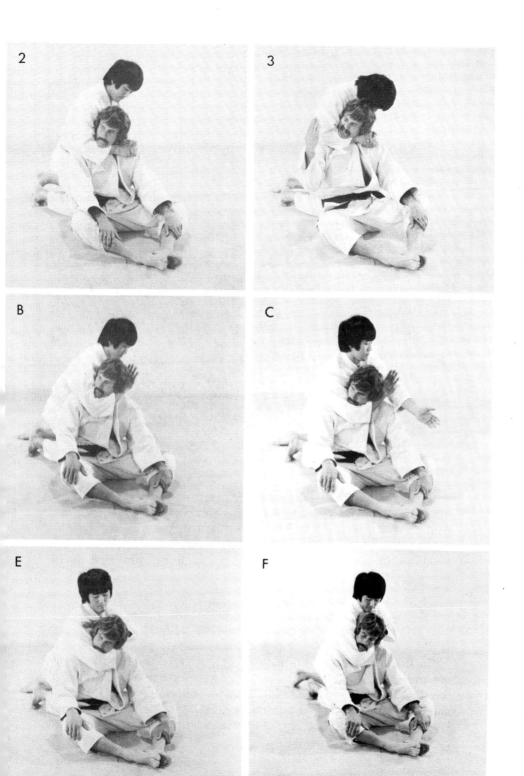

ARM BARS

Kansetsuwaza, or arm bars, are applied only to the elbow joint. Applied from a standing position or while on the ground, various methods are employed in securing the arm bar. But because of

D. Nelson attemps an arm bar

their extreme effectiveness and delicacy, these are restricted to black belts. If, on the other hand, a brown belt is engaged in a contest with a black belt, the brown belt may use an arm bar. No black belt, however, can use an arm bar on a brown belt except in elimination contests or championship matches as provided by International Judo Federation rules.

PRACTICAL EXPERIENCE

Go through each of the moves demonstrated in both the standing and grappling techniques and try to execute them according to the directions. While executing each technique, be mindful of the names of the throws and holds as well as their English equivalents. Whenever possible have a competent person check your form to correct it.

TEST YOURSELF

1. Give the two categories into which basic skills may fall.
2. In the first category of basic skills are listed salutations and methods of gripping, moving and falling. Discuss the reasoning behind each of these skills and describe how to execute each one.
3. The second category of basic skills is divided into standing techniques and grappling techniques. List by name (both English and Japanese) 10 throws as to their respective types and describe them.
4. What determines whether a technique is either a hand, hip or a foot technique?
5. Give the Japanese and English names of the five pinning holds and a brief description of each hold.
6. Give the Japanese and English names of the other two types of immobilizing mat techniques that are used, and describe their respective uses.

True-False Questions

1. The main reason behind bowing is to show one's respect and gratitude.
2. The bow is executed at the following times—answer each:
   A. When getting on or off the mat.
   B. When opponent does a very good throw.
   C. Before and after a match.
   D. Before and after practice sessions.
   E. After a superior in rank teaches a new technique.
3. The practitioner may only grab one way in a contest—right hand on opponent's lapel, left hand on opponent's right sleeve (if right-handed).
4. A person should move as fast as possible while practicing judo.
5. When moving, keep weight equally distributed.
6. Avoid bringing the feet together when moving.
7. Rolling falls are only used as a warmup drill.
8. *Shimewaza* can only be used by boys 12 or older.
9. *Kansetsuwaza* are only applied to elbows and knees by black belts.
10. *Kesagatame* is a very common *osaekomiwaza*.
11. There are only 15 throws in judo.
12. Judo throws are classified into hand, hip and foot techniques only.

Chapter IV

RANDORI

Despite the fact that 75 to 80 percent of judo training in a dojo consists of *randori*, little has been published on the subject. Many practical judo books have devoted less than two percent to the subject.

Yet the founder of judo, Jigoro Kano, put it this way: "*Randori* is practiced under conditions of actual contest. It includes throwing, choking, holding the opponent down and bending or twisting his arms .... The two combatants may use whatever methods they like, provided they do not hurt each other and obey the rules of judo concerning etiquette—which is essential to its proper working."

Randori is usually practiced by two judoka attacking and defending at will and need. Although it is usually an all-out effort by each participant to outdo the other, it can also be modified to meet specific needs. For example, beginning students are often encouraged to yield to rather than resist a technique initiated by an opponent.

Time limits may vary. Some dojos hold the sessions in five or 10 minute intervals, changing partners in-between. Others let the judoka decide how long to practice. In the latter instance, the length of a *randori* session may range from a minute to half-an-hour.

For the judo competitor, *randori* practice is not only a necessity, but the single most valuable judo practice method. Without stepping out on the mat and banging heads with skilled sparring partners, the judoka cannot properly prepare himself for tournament play or other self-defense situations. Experience in *randori*

will benefit the judoka by improving his attack patterns, decreasing movement time, and giving him first-hand experience of judo principles and conduct.

THE REAL THING

Ben Campbell, a past national judo champion, Pan-American Games gold medalist, Olympic competitor, physical educator and one of the premier judo coaches in the United States, hit the nail sharply on the head. "In kata practice, *uchikomi* or *suteigeiko*, the attack pattern is already known by both persons. In *randori*, you don't know when or how your opponent is going to attack . . . . You must keep alert at all times. In other words, *randori* is not a prearranged situation; it's the real thing."

If you're involved in an unexpected fight and get slugged in the face, the initial shock of the moment is a kind of trauma. In *randori*, there are likewise moments of trauma—physical and psychological (such as the anticipation of a stressful situation).

The more a judoka teaches himself to withstand such conditions, the better he becomes at coping with them. An example is Kazuo Shinohara, a 150-pound judo competitor. Sparring every day with college teammates who sometimes outweighed him by as much as 80 pounds, Shinohara was able, by his senior year, to hold his own with heavier opponents. Becoming captain of the powerful Meiji University team (which averaged 190 pounds), he was twice the university's grand champion.

Unlike *uchikomi* and *kata*, *randori* relies heavily on the play of emotions and the exertion of will. Attempting to up-end an opponent while at the same time fending off his attacks can be a very frustrating experience. One needs only to witness the determination on the faces of those practicing *randori* to appreciate the stress and strain involved.

During *randori*, the judoka does not talk. Nor does he think about anything other than compensating for his own inadequacies and overcoming his opponent. Practicing with a weaker player, the serious judoka does not let up, but chooses instead to practice and perfect a wider variety of techniques. Against an equally matched opponent, he bears down, constantly attacking and applying his most successful techniques. A stronger opponent demands that he concentrate on defensive technique, but he also looks for opportunities to apply the pressure of an aggressive attack. In every case, the sincere judoka seeks to make each of his movements into a work of art. In so doing, he maintains a single-minded goal: overcome the opponent.

Dr. Kano, extolling the benefits of *randori* in his speech at the 1932 Olympic Games, said, "Mental training in judo can be done by *kata* as well as *randori*, but more successfully by the latter. As *randori* is a competition between two persons using all the resources at their command and observing the prescribed rules of judo, both parties must remain wide awake, endeavoring to find weak points in the opponent, and being ready to attack whenever opportunity allows. Such an attitude of mind in devising means of attack tends to make the pupil earnest, sincere, thoughtful, cautious and deliberate in his performance. At the same time, one is trained for quick decision and prompt action, because in *randori*, unless one decides quickly and acts promptly, he will always lose his opportunity either to attack or defend . . . . Habituated to this kind of discipline, the judoka develops a high degree of mental composure—of poise. Exercise of the power of attention and observation in the gymnasium or place of training naturally develops such power, which is useful in daily life."

Like any other sport, judo relies heavily on strategy as the key to winning.

In 1965, Richard Walters handed a crumpled sheet of paper to a fellow teammate before stepping out on the mat. Uncrumpled, the note read as follows:

1. Left *osoto*
2. Right *ogoshi*
3. Right *ouchi*
4. *Newaza*, when possible

When the bout began, Walters applied the techniques he'd listed and, after some time, countered his opponent for half a point, then went on to pin him for another half-point and the win—exactly as he'd practiced it in *randori* and written it on the slip of paper. Walters later went on to win the openweight championship for the United States. This anecdote is but an example of how experienced competitors may use *randori* to prepare for tournament play.

Here are some suggestions for you, the student:

1. See how many times you can throw an opponent during a practice session.

2. Granting yourself one point each time you throw your sparring partner, see how many points you can score.

3. Determine how many times you can execute the same throw during one sparring session.

4. Practice throwing your partner as soon as you've gotten a grip on his gi.

5. Go through particular combinations until they become automatic.

6. Practice *randori* so hard you can no longer stand up.

Although there are many patterns of attack to be thought about, perhaps the best possible strategy in the long run is to develop the ability to act first and think and talk about it later.

Movement time is the period of time it takes to execute a specific movement. Obviously, the more skilled a participant is, the quicker he will be when it comes to executing. A properly applied technique grants the opponent a minimum amount of time in which to react, resist, counter or defend against the throw. The more you practice a technique, the faster you will be in employing it.

Learning how to deal with stress is vital to reducing movement time. According to Seymour Levine's article, "Stress and Behavior," in the January '71 issue of *Scientific American*, all effective behavior may be said to be contingent on the actor's ability to tolerate certain levels of stress. Because the *randori* is one long stress situation, the judoka may be able to discover for himself not only how effectively he is able to deal with stress, but determine as well the stress level which is optimum or ideal for himself. This would, perhaps, help to account for the international successes of Japanese judoka who rely heavily on *randori* in training.

The overall effect of *randori* in preparing the judoka for both tournament competition and everyday life was best described by Dr. Kano. "For devising means of defeating an opponent, the exercise of the power of imagination, of reasoning and judgment, is indispensable, and such power is naturally developed in *randori*. As the study of *randori* is the study of the relationship—mental and physical—existing between competing parties, hundreds of lessons may be derived . . . . In *randori*, we teach the pupil always to act on the fundamental principle of judo. No matter how physically inferior his opponent may seem to him—even if he can, by sheer strength, easily overcome the opponent—if he acts against this principle, the opponent will never be convinced of his defeat, whatever brutal strength has been used against him. The way to convince your opponent in an argument is not to push this or that advantage over him, be it from a position of power, knowledge or wealth—but to persuade him in accordance with the inviolable rule of reason or logic. This lesson—that persuasion not coercion is effective—is valuable in actual life, and we may learn this from the *randori.*"

PRACTICAL EXPERIENCE

Practice attacking and defending with an opponent who is doing likewise. Strive to throw the opponent even while he is doing his utmost to defend against your attack. Conversely, defend against the maneuvers of your opponent so as to avoid being thrown.

TEST YOURSELF

1. Give a definition of *randori* which includes the percentage of time that should be allotted to same. Name the categories of techniques employed, and explain the manner in which they are used.
2. Explain what is meant by the saying "*Randori* is *the real thing!*"
3. Explain how *randori* differs from *uchikomi* or *kata.*
4. Give the six suggestions listed as methods of practicing *randori.*
5. Explain what stress has to do with *randori.*

True-False Questions

1. *Randori* is the same as sparring in boxing.
2. *Randori* helps the judoka learn what he might expect in a contest.
3. The idea of *randori* is never to throw your opponent.
4. Strategy is virtually nonexistent in judo.

Chapter V

CONTEST RULES
OF THE INTERNATIONAL JUDO FEDERATION

The physical appearance of a sport is largely determined by the rules that govern its competition. With the emergence of judo as an international sport, sophisticated rules have been instituted to determine winners. In an effort to better the sport, these rules are constantly changing according to the judgments of the International Judo Federation (IJF). It is the job of IJF to see that the rules are both equitable and safe for its members.

Historically, efforts to decide on a winner often resulted in injury, or, in the case of jujitsu schools, even death. Many schools employed vigorous techniques and, using them in competition, caused permanent injuries. Even in the early days of Kodokan judo, leg locks, kicks and punches were used. Remnants of these practices are still found in *kata*, kicks and leg locks in *kime-no-kata*. Today, however, judo guards its integrity as a viable means of self-defense while embracing only those techniques and methods that allow it to be a safe sport.

Currently, judo rules have progressed from the *ippon* or full-point win and the *wazari* half-point-score-only system to the inclusion of a technical advantage points system. These scores, and the methods by which they are arrived at, will be discussed in more detail elsewhere.

The following set of rules was amended and approved by the IJF Montreal Congress in 1976, but first, here are a few simplified rules that illustrate and explain common referee signals. For a more in-depth understanding of the regulations, consult the regular set of rules following the illustrations.

REFEREE AND JUDGES' SIGNALS (1)

1. *Command to Start*
Verbal Signal: **HAJIME!**
Arm Signal: none
Implications: This command is given to begin or resume a match.

2. *Command to Stop or Wait*
Verbal Signal: **MATTE!**
Arm Signal: Arm is extended with palm facing outward. The command stops both match and time clock.
Implications: Given when contestants stray outside of contest area, commit an infraction of the rules, need to repair judo gi, or in the event of injury.

3. *Declaration of a Full Point*
Verbal Signal: **IPPON**
Arm Signal: Raise the right arm straight up. This signal to be given at the time the point is scored.
Implications: Announced when a throw has been executed with sufficient force, placing the opponent squarely on his back; also awarded for pinning the opponent on his back for 30 seconds; submission due to choke or arm bar; by win with two half-points, and/or combination with excessive infractions.

4. *Declaration of Half-Point*
Verbal Signal: **WAZARI**

Arm Signal: The right arm raised 90 degrees and held with fingers together palm down parallel with the floor. This signal is given at the time the half-point is won (by any method).

Implications: When the throw does not constitute an *ippon* or when the opponent has been held down for 25 to 29 seconds.

SIGNALS (2)

5. *Declaration of Near Half-Point*
Verbal Signal: **YUKO**

Arm Signal: Arm is held at 45 degrees away from the leg, palm downward.

Implications: Given when a throw is not quite a *wazari*, or if the opponent has been held down for 20 to 24 seconds.

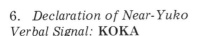

6. *Declaration of Near-Yuko*
Verbal Signal: **KOKA**

Arm Signal: Hand raised with back of palm close to shoulder, fingers together, palm facing outward.

Implications: Given usually when opponent has been thrown down with hip girdle contact which is insufficient to warrant the call of *yuko*; also given for any pin held for between 10 and 20 seconds.

7. *Declaration of Wrongly Awarded Score*
Verbal Signal: **none**

Arm Signal: As the appropriate wrong score signal is given with one arm, the other arm is waved several times high above the head. If a corrected score is to be given, it should be done immediately following the wave of the arm.

Implications: The two corner judges may feel a score was wrongly awarded.

GRAPPLING CALLS

8. *Declaration of Hold-Down*
Verbal Signal: **OSAEKOMI**

Arm Signal: The arm is extended downward at an angle of 30 degrees towards the contestants; palm held down, fingers extended, with the body bent slightly forward.

Implications: Given when one of the contestants has secured a pin; the opponent is down on his back and the person doing the pinning has his legs free.

9. *Declaration of Hold-Down Broken*
Verbal Signal: **OSAEKOMI TOKETA**

Arm Signal: Arm held in the same position as hold-down, but the thumb is held up, and the arm is waved from side to side several times.

Implications: That control has been lost by the attacker.

10. *Command to Stop Mat Work*
Verbal Signal: **SONO-MAMA**

Arm Signal: Both arms are extended and touch contestants, signaling that neither contestant should move. This is one of the few times that the referee touches contestants.

Implications: The command *mate* is usually used when contestants are standing; this signal is usually used when both contestants are off their feet: to signal infractions, check for injuries or to fix the judo gi.

11. *Command to Resume Mat Work*
Verbal Signal: **YOSHI**

Arm Signal: Once the contestants are properly positioned, the referee pats both contestants simultaneously.

Implications: Resume combat.

12. *Noncombat Call*
Verbal Signal: **none**

Arm Signal: Both hands are placed in front of the chest and are rotated around each other several times. Then the forefinger is pointed at the noncombative party or parties.

Implications: The first call is made when there is no attack for 15 to 20 seconds. The second call results in a shido—a score slightly higher than a *koka* score.

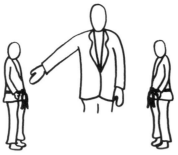

13. *Slight Infringement Call*
Verbal Signal: **SHIDO**
Arm Signal: Contestants may continue to move or be returned to the starting points before calling out the infringement. This is done by calling "*shido*," and pointing at the infringing party.

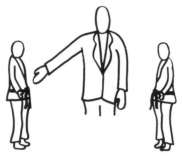

14. *Moderate Infringement Call*
Verbal Signal: **CHUI**
Arm Signal: Both contestants must be returned to the starting position unless in *newaza*. The referee points to the infringing party and calls out "*chui.*"
Implications: See Article 30—11-15. A score of chui is higher than a *yuko* or a near-*wazari*.

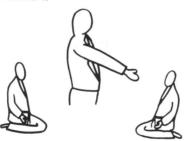

15. *Serious Infringement Call*
Verbal Signal: **KEIKOKU**
Arm Signal: The infringing party is placed in *seiza* or seated posi-

tion. The referee now steps between contestants, faces the infringing party and calls out "*keikoku.*"

Implications: See Article 30—16-25. Many infringements of this type deal with etiquette and safety. A *keikoku* call can only be counteracted by a score of *ippon* or *hasokumake.*

16. *Very Serious Infringement*

Verbal Signal: **HASOKUMAKE**

Arm Signal: Referee returns both contestants to the starting position, steps between them, points toward the infringing party and calls out "*hasokumake.*"

Implications: See Article 30—26. Both *keikoku* and *hasokumake* penalties must be agreed to by both corner judges. Disqualification.

17. *Request for Judges to Render a Decision*

Verbal Signal: **HANTEI**

Arm Signal: After waiting momentarily to prepare the judges, the referee shall call *"hantei."* Hand signal for this shall be the right hand extended vertically 180 degrees (as in *ippon*).

18. *Indication of a Draw Match*
Verbal Signal: **HIKIWAKE**
Arm Signal: Arm is raised above the head and briskly brought down with the thumb fully extended. The hand stops about chest high as the call *"hikiwake"* is given.
Implications: In some contests, provisions are made for overtime. In such cases, there is an immediate extension.

19. *Designation of Winning Contestant*
Verbal Signal: **WINNER**
Arm Signal: When both contestants and referee are in their proper positions, the referee raises the arm on the winning contestant's side and holds it up in the air at an angle of about 135 degrees.

CORNER JUDGES' SIGNALS

20. To indicate a difference of opinion with the referee, the judge raises his hand high above his head and waves it from side to side several times.

21. To indicate that in the opinion of the corner judge, the technique was executed within the boundaries of the competition area, the judge raises his arm from the floor to an angle of about 135 degrees and then moves it in a downward motion.

22. To indicate that a movement was executed outside the boun-

daries, the judge extends his arm, raises his thumb and waves back and forth across the boundary in question.

23. During a judge's decision, judges may indicate their preference by raising either a red or white flag to correspond with the contestant's sash. Where the judge awards a draw, both flags are raised.

CONTEST RULES OF THE INTERNATIONAL JUDO FEDERATION

WITH COMMENTARIES

ARTICLE 1. COMPETITION AREA

The competition area shall be a minimum of 14m x 14m and a maximum of 16m x 16m and shall be covered by tatami or a similarly acceptable material.

The competition area shall be divided into two zones. The demarcation between these two zones shall be called the danger area and shall be indicated by a colored area, generally red, approximately one metre wide forming part of or attached to the mat, parallel to the four sides of the competition area.

The area within and including the colored area shall be called the contest area and shall be always of a minimum of 9m x 9m or a maximum of 10m x 10m. The area outside the colored area shall be called the safety area, and shall never be less than 2 metres, 50 cms wide.

The above competition area must be mounted on a resilient platform.

COMMENTARY

Should two or more competition areas be placed on the same resilient platform as mentioned above, it is permissible for such adjoining safety areas to utilize mats common to both areas.

ARTICLE 2. COSTUME

The judo gi (judo costume) to be worn by the contestants shall comply with the following conditions:—

(a) The jacket shall be long enough to cover the hips and be tied at the waist by the belt.

(b) The sleeves shall be loose and long enough to cover more than half of the forearm (there should be an opening of between three and five centimeters between the cuff and the largest part of the forearm).

(c) The trousers shall be loose and long enough to cover more than half of the lower leg (there should be an opening of between five and eight centimeters between the bottom of the trousers and the largest part of the calf).

(d) The belt shall be tied with a square knot tight enough to prevent the jacket from being too loose and long enough to go twice around the body and leave about 20 to 30 cm protruding from each side of the knot when tied.

COMMENTARY

If the judo gi of a contestant does not comply with the article, the referee must order the contestant to change in the shortest possible time into a judo gi which does comply with the article.

If the referee suspects that the sleeves of a contestant's jacket are too short or too tight, he should raise both the contestant's arms forward to shoulder height in order to check in that position that they comply with paragraph (b) above.

Although not stated in the article, the referee should also ensure that the judo gi is uncolored, i.e., white or off-white.

Women contestants shall wear a white, or off-white, "long" short-sleeved tee-shirt under the judo gi jacket, tucked into the trousers.

ARTICLE 3. PERSONAL REQUIREMENTS

The contestants shall keep their nails cut short and shall not wear any metallic article because it may possibly injure or endanger the opponent.

Any contestant whose hair, in the opinion of the referee/judges, is so long as to risk causing inconvenience to the other contestant, shall be required to securely tie back the hair.

COMMENTARY

The phrase "metallic article" includes all "hard objects" which may cause injury.

It is not sufficient to cover a hard or metallic object such as a ring with tape or other covering.

The referee should also ensure that the personal hygiene of both contestants is of a high standard. For example, should a contestant arrive on the mat with dirty feet, he must be told to wash them, and anyone wearing a dirty judo gi must be made to change it.

If the contestant cannot or will not comply with this article, the referee shall declare his opponent the winner by "Kiken-Gachi."

ARTICLE 4. LOCATION

The contest shall be fought in the contest area. However, any technique applied when one or both of the contestants is outside the contest area shall not be recognized. That is to say that if one contestant shall have even one of his feet outside the contest area while standing, or more than half of his body outside the contest area whilst doing sutemi-waza (sacrifice throws) or ne-waza (groundwork), he shall be considered as being outside the contest area.

However, where one contestant throws his opponent outside the contest area but himself stays within the contest area long enough for the effectiveness of the technique to be clearly apparent, the technique shall be recognized.

When osaekomi has been called, it may continue—until the time allowed for the osaekomi expires or toketa is called—so long as at least one player has any part of his body touching the contest area (including the danger area).

COMMENTARY

As the colored danger area which defines the contest area from the safety area is immediately inside the boundary of the contest area, any contestant whose feet are still touching the colored danger area in the standing position should be considered as being still within the contest area.

When performing sutemi-waza, a throw is considered valid if the thrower has one-half or more of his body within the contest area. Therefore, neither foot of the thrower should leave the contest area before his back or hips touch the mat.

In ne-waza, the action is valid and may continue so long as both contestants have at least half of their bodies inside the contest area.

If the thrower falls outside the contest area whilst making a throw, the action will only be considered for point-scoring purposes where the opponent's body touches the mat before the thrower's. Therefore, if a thrower's knee, hand or any other part of his body touches the ground before his opponent's, any result obtained thereby should be disregarded.

If, however, during the course of an attack such as o-uchi-gari or ko-uchi-gari, the foot or leg of the thrower leaves the contest area and moves over the mats of the safety area, the action should be considered valid for point-scoring purposes so long as the thrower does not place any weight upon the foot or leg while it is out of the contest area.

Once the contest has started, the contestants may only leave the competition area if given permission to do so by the referee. Permission will only be given in very exceptional circumstances, such as the necessity to change a judo gi which does not comply with article two or has become damaged or soiled.

ARTICLE 5. POSITION AT START OF CONTEST

The contestants shall stand facing each other at the center of the contest area and approximately 4m apart and shall make a standing bow.

The contest shall begin immediately after the announcement of hajime (begin) by the referee and shall always begin with both contestants in the standing position.

NO COMMENTARY

ARTICLE 6. START AND END OF CONTEST

The referee shall announce hajime (begin) in order to start the contest after the contestants have bowed to each other.

The referee shall announce sore-made (that is all) at the end of the contest.

At the end of the contest, the contestants shall return to the places in which they started the contest and standing facing each other shall again make a standing bow after the referee has indicated the result of the contest.

NO COMMENTARY

ARTICLE 7. RESULT

The result of a contest shall be judged only on the basis of nage-waza (throwing techniques) and katame-waza (grappling techniques).

NO COMMENTARY

ARTICLE 8. TERMINATION BY IPPON (full point)

The contest shall immediately end if and when one of the contestants scores ippon (full point).

NO COMMENTARY

ARTICLE 9. ENTRY INTO NE-WAZA (groundwork)

The contestants shall be able to change from the standing position to ne-waza (groundwork) in the

133

following cases, but should the employment of the technique not be continuous, the referee may, at his discretion, order both contestants to resume the standing position.

  (a) When a contestant after obtaining some result by a throwing technique changes without interruption into ne-waza (groundwork) and takes the offensive.

  (b) When one of the contestants falls to the ground, following the unsuccessful application of a throwing technique, the other may follow him to the ground; or when one of the contestants is unbalanced and is liable to fall to the ground after the unsuccessful application of a throwing technique, the other may take advantage of his opponent's unbalanced position to take him to the ground.

  (c) When one contestant obtains some considerable effect by applying a shime-waza (strangle) or kansetsu-waza (a lock) in the standing position and then changes without interruption to ne-waza (groundwork).

  (d) When one contestant takes his opponent down into ne-waza (groundwork) by the particularly skillful application of movement which although resembling a throwing technique does not fully qualify as such.

  (e) In any other case, where one contestant may fall down or be about to fall down, not covered by the preceding subsections of this article, the other contestant may take advantage of his opponent's position to go into ne-waza (groundwork).

COMMENTARY

If one contestant tries to apply ju-ji-gatame or any similar technique from the standing position and the result is not immediately apparent, the referee shall call matte.

For further comments see Commentary No. 6 of Article 31.

ARTICLE 10. DURATION

The duration of the contest shall be arranged in advance and shall be not less than three minutes and not more than 20 minutes. This arranged time may, however, be extended in certain special cases.

The time elapsed between the call of "Matte" and "Hajime" and between "Sono-mama" and "Yoshi" by the referee shall not count as part of the duration of the contest.

COMMENTARY

All contestants shall be allowed a recuperation period of at least the same duration as the contest in which they are about to compete, to be timed if necessary from the moment that their previous contest ended.

ARTICLE 11. TIME SIGNAL

The end of the time allotted for the contest shall be indicated to the referee by the ringing of a bell or other similar audible method.

NO COMMENTARY

ARTICLE 12. TECHNIQUE COINCIDING WITH TIME SIGNAL

Any throwing technique which is applied simultaneously with the bell (or other method of indicating the end of the time allotted) shall be recognized, and when an osaekomi (holding) is simillarly announced simultaneously with the signal bell, etcetera, the time allotted for the contest shall be extended until either ippon is scored or the referee announces toketa (hold broken).

Further, any technique applied after the ringing of the bell or other device to indicate the expiry of the time of the contest shall not be valid, even if the referee has not at that time called sore-made.

COMMENTARY

Although a throwing technique may be applied simultaneously with the bell, if the referee decides that it will not be effective immediately, he should announce sore-made.

ARTICLE 13. SONO-MAMA

In any case where the referee wishes to stop the contest (e.g., in order to adjust the dress of the players, or to address either of them without causing a change in their positions), he will call "sono-mama." To recommence the contest, he will call "yoshi."

COMMENTARY

Whenever the referee applies the rule and action of sono-mama, he must be particularly careful that there is no change of relative position of both the contestants.

ARTICLE 14. RESPONSIBILITY

All actions and decisions taken in accordance with the majority of three rule as in Article 26 by the referee and judges shall be final and without appeal.

NO COMMENTARY

ARTICLE 15. OFFICIALS

In general, the contest shall be conducted by one referee and two judges. However, in certain circumstances it may be permissible to have one referee and one judge or even just one referee.

COMMENTARY

The referee and judges shall be assisted by a contest recorder, who shall visibly record in writing or by means of a suitable apparatus, all scores and penalties announced by the referee, as accepted or modified by the judges under the majority of three rule. At the end of the contest, the contest recorder shall, if requested, indicate to the referee and judges the total scores and/or penalties awarded to each contestant.

When recording penalties, the contest recorder must ensure that only one penalty is shown recorded against any one contestant at a time. For example, if one contestant is penalized with a shido and is then given a further penalty of a chui or a keikoku, the earlier lesser offense must always be removed from the score once the new offense has been added.

ARTICLE 16. POSITION AND FUNCTION OF REFEREE

The referee shall stay generally within the contest area and has the sole responsibility for conducting the contest and administering the judgment.

COMMENTARY

In general, and from time to time, the referee and judges shall observe that the scores recorded by the contest recorder are correct with the scores that have been announced.

ARTICLE 17. POSITION AND FUNCTION OF JUDGES

The judges shall assist the referee and shall be positioned opposite each other at two corners outside the contest area.

Should a contestant be permitted to leave the competition area after the start of the contest (Commentary to Article 4), one judge must go and remain with him until he returns to the competition area.

COMMENTARY

As the judges will be seated on the safety area, they must be particularly alert to the need to remove both themselves and their chairs should it appear that one or more contestants may leave the contest area at the place where they are sitting.

In general and from time to time, the referee and judges shall observe that the scores recorded by the contest recorder are correct with the scores that have been announced.

ARTICLE 18. IPPON (full point)

The referee shall announce ippon (full point) when in his opinion a throwing or grappling technique applied by a contestant merits the score of ippon, and after stopping the contest shall return both contestants to the places in which they began the contest.

In the case where both contestants score a result which would merit ippon simultaneously (for example, strangling techniques), the referee shall announce hiki-wake (draw) and the contestants shall have the right to fight the contest again where necessary.

COMMENTARY

Should the referee call "ippon" during ne-waza in error and the contestants therefore separate, the referee and judges may, in accordance with Article 14, replace the contestants into as close to their original position as possible and restart the contest, if so doing will rectify an injustice to one of the contestants.

Where a hiki-wake decision has been awarded in accordance with this article and only one contestant wishes to exercise his right to fight the contest again and the other contestant declines, the contestant who wishes to fight again should be declared the winner by ippon.

ARTICLE 19. WAZA-ARI (almost ippon)

The referee shall announce waza-ari (almost ippon) when in his opinion the technique applied by a contestant merits the score of waza-ari (almost ippon).

Should one contestant gain a second waza-ari (almost ippon), the referee shall announce instead waza-ari awasete ippon (two waza-aris score ippon), and after stopping the contest, shall return both contestants to the places in which they began the contest.

NO COMMENTARY

ARTICLE 20. YUKO (almost waza-ari)

The referee shall announce "yuko" (almost waza-ari) when in his opinion the technique applied by the contestant merits the score of yuko.

Should either contestant score two or further yukos, then the referee shall announce them as they are scored but shall not stop the contest for that reason.

Regardless of how many yukos are announced, no amount will be considered as being equal to a waza-ari. The total number announced will be recorded and used in arriving at the decision whenever a contest is not won by ippon.

NO COMMENTARY

ARTICLE 21. KOKA (almost yuko)

The referee shall announce "koka" (almost yuko) when in his opinion the technique applied by the contestant merits the score of koka (almost yuko).

Should either contestant score two or further kokas, then the referee shall announce them as they are scored but shall not stop the contest for that reason.

Regardless of how many kokas are announced, no amount will be considered as being equal to a yuko or waza-ari. The total number announced will be recorded and used in arriving at the decision whenever a contest is not won by ippon.

NO COMMENTARY

ARTICLE 22. SOGO-GACHI (compound win)

The referee shall stop the contest and following the usual procedure indicate the winner after announcing sogo-gachi (compound win) in the following cases:—

Where one contestant has gained a waza-ari (almost ippon) and his opponent subsequently receives a penalty of keikoku (warning) or similarly where one contest whose opponent has already received a penalty of keikoku (warning) is subsequently himself awarded a waza-ari (almost ippon).

NO COMMENTARY

ARTICLE 23. OSAEKOMI (holding)

The referee shall announce osaekomi (holding) when in his opinion one contestant is successfully holding the other by a holding technique. The referee shall immediately announce toketa (hold broken) at any time after the announcement of osaekomi (holding) when he considers the hold to be broken.

COMMENTARY

In any case of doubt, the referee should ascertain from the time-keepers and then inform the judges of the length of time elapsed between the calls of osaekomi and toketa.

ARTICLE 24. JUDGES' UNSOLICITED OPINIONS

A judge will indicate his opinion, by making the appropriate official signal, whenever his opinion differs from that of the referee. When both judges indicate the same opinion, the judge closest to the referee shall immediately approach him requesting that he stop the contest and rectify the decision. If the second judge does not hold the same opinion as the first judge, he shall make no signal and the decision of the referee shall prevail.

COMMENTARY

If at any time, the referee and two judges all hold differing opinions the referee must make his final decision on the following basis:

(a) should the referee express an opinion of a higher degree than that of the two judges on a technical results or a penalty, he shall adjust his evaluation to that of the judge having expressed the highest evaluation.

(b) should the referee express an opinion of a lower degree than that of the two judges on a technical result or a penalty, he shall adjust his evaluation to that of the judge having expressed the lowest evaluation.

(c) should a judge express an opinion of a higher degree and the other judge an opinion of a lower degree than that of the referee, the referee shall maintain his opinion.

ARTICLE 25. HANTEI (request for decision)

The referee shall announce sore-made (that is all), stop the contest and return both contestants to their original starting places should the time allotted for the contest expire without there having been a score of ippon.

Should the recorded scores indicate an advantage for either contestant on the following scale—one waza-ari wins over any number of yukos or kokas, and when no waza-ari has been scored, one or more yukos wins over any number of kokas (see Article 36(d))—the referee, having confirmed which contestant has won, will so indicate by raising his hand toward the winner.

Should the unrecorded scores either indicate no scores or be exactly the same under each of the headings (waza-ari, yuko, koka), then the referee shall call "hantei," while raising a hand high in the air. The judges shall in response to this signal, raise either the white or red flag above their heads in order to indicate which contestant they consider merits the decision. To indicate hiki-wake (draw), the judges shall raise the red and white flags simultaneously.

NO COMMENTARY

ARTICLE 26. DECLARATION OF DECISION

The referee shall add his own opinion to that indicated by the two judges and shall declare the results according to the majority decision of all three.

When there is only one judge, the referee shall take into consideration the opinion of the judge before announcing the results.

COMMENTARY

Where the referee has a differing opinion from that of the two judges after having called hantei, he may delay giving his decision in order to discuss with them their reasons and thereafter once again shall call hantei, and this time must give his decision based upon the majority of three.

Once the referee has announced the result of the contest to the contestants, it will not be possible for the referee to change this decision once he has left the competition area.

Should the referee award the victory to the wrong contestant in error, the two judges must ensure that he change the erroneous decision before he leaves the contest area.

ARTICLE 27. APPLICATION OF MATTE (wait)

The referee shall announce matte (wait) in order to stop the contest temporarily in the following cases and to recommence the contest shall announce hajime (begin).

(a) When one or both of the contestants go outside the contest area.

(b) When one or both of the contestants perform or are about to perform one of the prohibited acts.

137

(c) When one or both of the contestants are injured or taken ill.

(d) When it is necessary for one or both of the contestants to adjust their costumes.

(e) When during ne-waza (groundwork) there is no apparent progress and the contestants lie still in a position such as ashi-garami (entangled legs).

(f) When one contestant remains in, or from ne-waza regains, a standing position and lifts his opponent, who is on his back with his leg(s) around any part of the standing contestant, clear of the mat.

(g) When in any other case that the referee deems it necessary to do so.

When the referee has called "matte," the contestant(s) must either stand if being spoken to or having their clothing adjusted, or may sit cross-legged if a lengthy delay is envisaged. Only when receiving medical attention should a contestant be permitted to adopt any other position.

COMMENTARY

Should the referee call "matte" in error during the ne-waza and the contestants therefore separate, the referee and judges may in accordance with Article 14 replace the contestants into as close to their original position as possible and restart the contest, if so doing will rectify an injustice to one of the contestants.

ARTICLE 28. DECISION AFTER PROHIBITED ACTS

Whenever a contest has been decided by hansoku (prohibited act), fusen (default), kiken (withdrawal), injury or accident, the referee shall indicate to the contestants the winner of the contest, or if the decision is hiki-wake (draw), the referee shall so announce the result.

NO COMMENTARY

ARTICLE 29. OFFICIAL SIGNALS

The officials shall make gestures as indicated below when taking the following actions:—

(a) The Referee

i   Ippon. Raise one of his hands high above his head.

ii   Waza-ari. Raise one of his hands, palm down, sideways from his body at shoulder height.

iii   Yuko. Raise one of his arms, palm downwards, sideways, 45 degrees from his body.

iv   Koka. Raise one of his arms bent with thumb towards the shoulder and elbow at hip level.

v   Osaekomi. Point his arm out away from his body down towards the contestants, while facing the contestants and bending his body towards them.

vi   Osaekomi toketa. Raise one of his hands to the front and wave it from right to left quickly two or three times.

vii   Hiki-wake. Raise one of his hands high in the air and bring it down to the front of his body (with thumb edge up) and hold it there for a while.

viii   Matte. Raise one of his hands to shoulder height and with the arm approximately parallel to the tatami, display the flattened palm of his hand with the fingers up to the time keeper.

ix   To indicate a technique not considered valid, raise one of his hands above his head to the front and wave it from right to left two or three times.

x   To indicate that in his opinion either or both of the contestants are guilty of "noncombativity," raise both his hands to chest height in front of his body and rotate both hands around each other in the direction of the offending contestant or contestants.

xi   When awarding a penalty to one or the other contestant, the referee should point toward the contestant concerned with a finger extending from a closed fist.

xii   To indicate cancellation of a wrongly awarded score, repeat the signal erroneously made with one hand while raising the other hand above his head to the front and waving it from right to left, two or three times. Note: If an amended score is to be awarded, it should be made as soon as possible after this cancellation signal.

xiii To indicate the winner of the contest, raise his hand above shoulder height towards the winner.

(b) The Judges

i   To indicate that he considers a contestant has stayed within the contest area, the judge shall raise one of his hands up in the air and bring it down to shoulder height along the boundary line of the contest area generally with the thumb upwards and momentarily hold it there.

ii   To indicate that in his opinion one of the contestants is out of the contest area, the judge shall raise one of his hands to shoulder height along the boundary line of the contest area generally with the thumb edge upwards and wave it from right to left several times.

iii   To indicate that in his opinion a score awarded by the referee, as in Article 29(a) above, has no validity whatsoever, the judge shall raise one of his hands above his head to the front and wave it from right to left, two or three times.

iv   To indicate a different opinion from that indicated by the referee, the judge shall make any of the signals in (a) as are appropriate in order to comply with Article 24.

COMMENTARY

The above signals should generally be held for a minimum of three seconds.

ARTICLE 30. PROHIBITED ACTS

All the following acts are forbidden:

Slight infringements—normally penalized by SHIDO:

(i)   To intentionally avoid taking hold of the opponent in order to prevent action in the contest.

(ii)   To adopt an excessively defensive attitude.

(iii) To hold continually the opponent's collar, lapel or sleeve on the same side with both hands or the opponent's belt or the bottom of his jacket with either or both hands in a standing position, to continually hold the opponent's sleeve end(s) for a defensive purpose.

(iv)   To insert a finger or fingers inside the opponent's sleeve or the bottom of his trousers or to grasp by "screwing up" his sleeve.

(v)   To stand continually with the fingers of one or both hands interlocked in order to prevent action in the contest.

(vi)   To intentionally disarrange his own judo gi (judo costume) or to untie or retie the belt or the trousers without the referee's permission.

(vii) To take hold of the opponent's leg or foot in a standing position, grasp the foot (feet), the the leg(s), the pant leg(s) with one/both hands(s), except to simultaneously apply a throwing technique.

(viii) To wind the end of the belt or jacket around any part of the opponent's body.

(ix)   To take the opponent's judo gi (judo costume) in the mouth or to put a hand or arm or foot or leg directly on the opponent's face.

(x)   To maintain (not let go) whilst lying on the back a hold with the legs round the neck and armpits of the opponent when the opponent succeeds in standing or gets to his knees in a position from which he could lift up the contestant.

Moderate infringements—normally penalized by CHUI:

(xi)   To apply the action of dojime (leg scissors) to the opponent's trunk, neck or head.

(xii) To kick with the knee or foot the hand or arm of the opponent in order to make him release his grasp.

(xiii) To put a foot or leg in the opponent's belt, collar or lapel or to bend back the opponent's finger or fingers in order to break the opponent's grip.

(xiv) To pull the opponent down in order to start ne-waza (groundwork).

(xv)   To go outside the contest area from the standing position while applying a technique started in the contest area.

Serious infringements—normally penalized by KEIKOKU:

(xvi) To intentionally, from a standing position, go outside the contest area or intentionally force the opponent to go outside the contest area.

(xvii) To attempt to throw the opponent with kawazu-gake. (Kawazu-gake is a technique of non-Judo origin performed by winding one leg around the opponent's leg whilst facing more or less in the same direction as the opponent and falling backward onto him.)

(xviii) To apply kansetsu-waza (joint locks) anywhere other than the elbow joint.

(xix) To apply any action which might injure the neck or spinal vertebrae of the opponent.

(xx) To lift off the mat an opponent who is lying on his back in order to drive him back into the mat.

(xxi) To sweep the opponent's supporting leg from the inside when the opponent is applying a technique such as harai-goshi (sweeping loin).

(xxii) To attempt to apply any technique outside the contest area.

(xxiii) To disregard the referee's instructions.

(xxiv) To make unnecessary calls, remarks or gestures derogatory to the opponent during the contest.

(xxv) To make any other action which may injure or endanger the opponent or may be against the spirit of judo.

Very serious infringements—normally penalized by HANSOKU-MAKE:

(xxvi) To intentionally fall backwards when the other contestant is clinging to your back and when either contestant has control of the other's movement.

(xxvii) To dive into the mat, head first whilst executing an uchimata, harai-goshi or technique of like nature.

(xxviii) To apply kanibasami or scissors throw and cause injury.

The above division of infringements into four groups is intended as a guide, to give a clearer understanding to all, of the relative penalties normally awarded for committing the applicable prohibited act. Referees and judges are authorized to award penalties according to the "intent" or "situation" and in the best interests of the sport.

Any contestant who performs or attempts to perform any of the above acts shall be liable for disqualification or other disciplinary action by the referee in accordance with these rules.

COMMENTARY

Not withstanding Article 4 (Location), if the referee has the opinion that a contestant has intentionally and against the spirit of judo thrown his opponent out of the contest area, the contestant should be penalized.

In relation to paragraph (ii) of this article, a state of noncombativity may be taken to exist when in general for 20 to 30 seconds there have been no attacking moves on the part of one of either or both contestants. This period may be prolonged or shortened depending upon the circumstances.

In relation to paragraph (xxvii) of this article, the uchimata and harai-goshi throws should be counted if the opponents maintain body contact continually throughout the throw without a separation beyond 40 degrees, since there is no danger to the thrower.

In relation to paragraph (xxviii) of this article, when no injury results, then a lesser penalty of keikoku may be given.

ARTICLE 31. PENALTIES

The referee shall declare shido (note), chui (caution), keikoku (warning) or hansoku-make (disqualification) according to the gravity of any infringement of the regulations in Article 30. In general, a simple repetition of an infringement in one of the above-mentioned categories shall merit a penalty of the next highest category.

If shido (note) is announced to one contestant, the other shall be regarded as having scored koka (almost yuko); if chui (caution) is announced to one contestant, the other shall be regarded as having scored yuko (almost waza-ari), and if keikoku (warning) is awarded to one contestant, the other shall be considered as having been awarded waza-ari (almost ippon).

Should the referee award chui (caution), he shall temporarily stop the contest, return the contestants to the standing position in which they started the contest, and announce chui (caution) whilst pointing toward the contestant who committed the prohibited act.

Should the referee decide to award keikoku (warning), he shall temporarily stop the contest, and shall generally return the contestants to the standing position in which they started the contest and shall announce keikoku whilst pointing toward the contestant who committed the prohibited act.

However, if in ne-waza, it is the contestant who is in a disadvantageous position who commits the offense meriting a penalty, the referee shall announce "sono-mama," apply the penalty and then recommence the contest by announcing "yoshi."

If it is the contestant who is in the advantageous position who commits the offense meriting a penalty, the referee shall announce "matte," return the contestants to the standing position in which they started the contest, award the penalty (and any score should an osaekomi have been in progress), and then recommence the contest by announcing "hajime."

Should the referee award hansoku-make, in accordance with paragraph 7 of the commentary to this article, he shall return the contestants to the standing position in which they started the contest, step forward between them, face the competitor concerned and while pointing at him announce "hansoku-make." He shall then step back to his original position and raise his hand in the signal to indicate the winner of the contest.

COMMENTARY

(1) Shido is generally given to any contestant who is about to infringe or who has already committed a very slight infringement of Article 30 (Prohibited Acts).

Chui is generally given to any contestant who repeats a very slight infringement or commits a moderate infringement of Article 30.

Keikoku is generally given to any contestant who repeats a moderate infringement or commits a serious infringement of Article 30.

Hansoku-make is generally given to any contestant who repeats a serious infringement or who commits a very grave infringement of Article 30.

(2) Where both contestants infringe the rules at the same time, each should be awarded a penalty according to the degree of the infringement.

(3) Where both contestants have already been awarded keikoku and subsequently each receives a further penalty, they should both be declared hansoku-make. Nonetheless, the officials may make their final decision in this matter in accordance with Article 41 (Situations not covered by these rules).

(4) Where a contestant infringes paragraphs "xv" or "xvi" of Article 30, the penalty awarded should be as follows:—

    (a) Where one contestant deliberately leaves the contest area or pretends to apply a technique in order to leave the contest area, the penalty given should be keikoku.

    (b) Where a contestant deliberately forces his opponent out of the contest area (including the case referred to in the commentary in Article 30), the penalty should be keikoku.

    (c) If a contestant leaves the contest area due to his own efforts to upset his opponent's balance the penalty awarded should be chui. However, if he leaves the contest area as the result of an action by his opponent, he should not be penalized.

(5) The first warning by the referee (Article 29(a)x) that he considers that either or both of the contestants are guilty of noncombativity should not entail the awarding of any penalty to the contestants so warned. Subsequent warnings should entail awarding penalties in accordance with the article to which this commentary applies.

(6) (a) Where one contestant pulls his opponent down into ne-waza not in accordance with Article 9 and his opponent does not take advantage of this to continue into ne-waza, the referee shall call matte, stop the contest and award chui to the contestant who has infringed Article 9.

    (b) Where one contestant pulls his opponent down into ne-waza not in acordance with the rules of Article 9 and his opponent takes advantage of this to continue into ne-waza, the contest should be allowed to continue, but the referee should award chui to the contestant who has infringed Article 9.

(7) Before awarding keikoku or hansoku-make, the referee must consult with the judges and make the decision in accordance with the majority of three.

(8) Penalties are not cumulative. Each penalty must be awarded at its own value.

The awarding of any second or subsequent penalty automatically cancels any earlier penalty. Whenever a contestant has already been penalized, any succeeding penalties for the contestant must always be awarded at least in the next higher value than his existing penalty.

ARTICLE 32. ASSESSMENT OF IPPON

The decision of ippon (full point) shall be given in the following cases:—

(a) Nage-waza (throwing techniques)

    i When the contestant applying a technique or countering his opponent's attacking technique throws his opponent largely on his back with considerable force or speed.

(b) Katame-waza (grappling techniques)

    i When one contestant says maitta (I give up) or taps his own or his opponent's body or the mat with his hand or foot twice or more.

    ii When one contestant holds the other, who is unable to get away, for 30 seconds, after the announcement of osaekomi (holding).

    iii Where the effect of a technique or shime-waza (strangle) or kansetsu-waza (lock) is sufficiently apparent.

COMMENTARY

Where one contestant, who is holding his opponent by an osaekomi-waza which has been "called," changes without loss of control into another or succeeding osaekomi-waza, the time shall be allowed to continue until ippon has been declared or the opponent succeeds in escaping.

Although a contestant who deliberately lands in a form of "bridge" (head and heels with most of his body off the ground) after having been thrown can be said to have prevented his opponent from complying with Article 32(a)i above, the referee should still generally award ippon in order to discourage this technique.

ARTICLE 33. ASSESSMENT OF WAZA-ARI

The decision of waza-ari (almost ippon) shall be given in the following cases:—

(a) Nage-waza (throwing techniques)

When a contestant applying a throwing technique is not completely successful (for example, the technique is lacking in any one of the three elements of: largely on his back, force or speed) and does not quite merit the score of ippon.

(b) Osaekomi-waza (holding techniques)

When one contestant is holding another as in Article 32(b)ii for 25 seconds or more but less than 30 seconds.

COMMENTARY

Where one contestant tries tomoe-nage but is temporarily unsuccessful and then after an appreciable time whilst still on his back subsequently succeeds in completing tomoe-nage, he shall only be able to score a maximum of waza-ari because the throw is now being done from a lying and not a standing position.

ARTICLE 34. ASSESSMENT OF YUKO

The decision of yuko (almost waza-ari) shall be given in the following cases:—

(a) Nage-waza (throwing techniques)

When a contestant applying a throwing technique is only partially successful—for example, is lacking more than is required to score waza-ari, one of the three elements of: largely on the back, force or speed, and does not quite merit the score of waza-ari.

(b) Osaekomi-waza (holding techniques)

When one contestant is holding another, as in Article 32(b)ii, for 20 seconds or more, but less than 25 seconds.

NO COMMENTARY

ARTICLE 35. ASSESSMENT OF KOKA

The decision of koka (almost yuko) shall be given in the following cases:—

(a) Nage-waza (throwing techniques)

When a contestant makes a throwing technique which is not successful, but with some force or speed puts his opponent on to his side, thigh(s), stomach or buttocks and does not quite merit the score of yuko.

(b) Osaekomi-waza (holding techniques)

When one contestant is holding another, as in Article 32(b)ii, for 10 seconds or more but less than 20 seconds.

COMMENTARY

Throwing an opponent on to his knee(s), hand(s) or elbow(s) will only be counted as the same as any other attack. Simiarly, an osaekomi of up to nine seconds will be counted the same as an attack.

ARTICLE 36. ASSESSMENT OF YUSEI-GACHI

The decision of yusei-gachi (superiority win) shall generally be given in the following cases:—

(a) Where there has been a score of waza-ari (almost ippon) or a penalty of keikoku (warning).

(b) Where there has been a score of yuko (almost waza-ari) or a penalty of chui (caution).

(c) Where there has been a score of koka (almost yuko) or a penalty of shido (note).

(d) Where all scores as recorded in Article 25 are equal for both contestants, the yusei-gachi shall be given to the contestant who has the least severe penalty recorded against him.

(e) Where there is a recognizable difference in the attitude during the contest or in the skill and effectiveness of technique.

COMMENTARY

(a) The criteria for deciding where yusei-gachi wins should be dispensed with entirely or should be applied according to (a), (b), (c), (d) or (e) above, are the responsibility of the organizing committee for each particular event and officials should ascertain before taking their places on the mat under which conditions yusei-gachi is to be given.

ARTICLE 37. ASSESSMENT OF HIKI-WAKE

The decision of hiki-wake (draw) shall be given when there is no positive score and where it is impossible to judge the superiority of either contestant in accordance with Article 36 above within the time allotted for the contest.

NO COMMENTARY

ARTICLE 38. ASSESSMENT OF HANSOKU-MAKE

The decision of hansoku-make (disqualification) should be given:—

(a) Where one contestant has had the penatly of keikoku (warning) awarded against him and then receives a further penalty.

(b) Where any act on the part of one contestant gravely infringes Article 30 above (Prohibited Acts) as, for example, where any act on his part may injure or endanger his opponent or any remark or gesture, etcetera, of his is considered to be contrary to the principles of judo.

COMMENTARY

The decision as to whether a contestant should be disqualified from a tournament or competition can only be taken by or under the authority of the Directing Committee of the organization for which the tournament or competition is being held.

ARTICLE 39. DEFAULT AND WITHDRAWAL

The decision of fusen-gachi (win by default) shall be given to any contestant whose opponent does not appear for his contest.

The decision of kiken-gachi (win by withdrawal) shall be given to any contestant whose opponent withdraws from the competition during the contest.

NO COMMENTARY

ARTICLE 40. INJURY, ILLNESS OR ACCIDENT

In every case where a competition is stopped because of injury to either or both of the contestants, the referee and judges may permit a maximum time of five minutes to the injured player(s) for recuperation.

The decision of kachi (win), make (loss), hiki-wake (draw), where one contestant is unable to continue because of injury, illness or accident during the contest, shall be given by the referee after consultation with the judges according to the following clauses:—

(a) Injury

   i Where the cause of the injury is attributed to the injured contestant, he shall lose the contest.

   ii Where the cause of the injury is attributed to the uninjured contestant, the uninjured contestant shall lose the contest.

   iii Where it is impossible to attribute the cause of injury to either contestant, the decision of hiki-wake (draw) may be given.

(b) Sickness

Generally, where one contestant is taken sick during a contest and is unable to continue, he shall lose the contest.

(c) Accident

Where an accident occurs which is due to an outside influence, the decision hiki-wake (draw) shall be given.

COMMENTARY

Should a doctor advise a contestant to withdraw from a competition and the contestant does not wish to do so, the referee should ensure that the contestant first signs a release or waiver of responsibility.

ARTICLE 41. SITUATIONS NOT COVERED BY THE RULES

Where any situation arises which is not covered by these rules, it shall be dealt with and a decision given by the referee after consultation with the judges.

NO COMMENTARY

PRACTICAL EXPERIENCE

Attend a tournament and mentally assess and apply the rules as you watch the matches. See if your decision is similar to that of the referee. If it differs, *find out why!*

TEST YOURSELF

Give the definition of the following terms.

1. Hajime (article 5)
2. Sore-made (article 6)
3. Nage-waza (article 7)
4. Katame-waza (article 7)
5. Ippon (article 8)
6. Ne-waza (article 9)
7. Sutemi-waza (article 4)
8. Shime-waza (article 9c)
9. Osaekomi (articles 12 and 23)
10. Toketa (article 12)
11. Sono-mama (article 13)
12. Yoshi (article 13)
13. Ippon (article 18)
14. Wazari (article 19)
15. Yuko (article 20)
16. Koka (article 21)
17. Sogo-gachi (article 22)
18. Hantei (article 25)
19. Hikiwake (article 26)
20. Yusei-gachi (article 26)
21. Matte (article 27)
22. Hansoku (article 28)
23. Fusen (article 28)
24. Kiken (article 28)
25. Shido (article 31)
26. Chui (article 31)
27. Keikoku (article 31)
28. Hansoku-make (article 31)
29. Kensetsu-waza (article 32)
30. Maitta (article 32)
31. Kachi (article 40)
32. Make (article 40)

True-False Questions

1. The command *hajime* will begin the match.
2. *Ippon* shall be given for the following—answer each:
   a. When the contestant skillfully throws his opponent largely on his back with considerable force or impetus.
   b. When one opponent says *maitta* or taps twice or more with hand or foot to give up.
   c. When the opponent is held to the mat and controlled for 25 seconds.
   d. Where the effect of a technique of *shime-waza* or *kansetsu-waza* is sufficiently apparent.
   e. When an overtime decision is granted by the referee and judges to one contestant for being the most aggressive.
   f. When a contestant applying a throw lifts his opponent eight feet off the mat.
3. The following acts are prohibited in judo—answer each:
   a. To apply any action which may injure the neck or spinal vertebrae.
   b. To throw the opponent as hard as possible.
   c. To choke the opponent into unconsciousness.
   d. To apply leg scissors to the opponent's trunk.
   e. To intentionally go outside mat area to avoid an attack.
   f. To take hold of the opponent's leg or foot in order to change to *ne-waza* unless doing so while attempting the execution of a technique.

Chapter VI

PLANNING TO WIN

HOW DO WE PLAN OUT A STRATEGY FOR WINNING?

In planning an approach to winning, either in competition or practice, the strengths and weaknesses of both an opponent and one's self must be taken into account.

Take football. A constant battle of strategy and counterstrategy is one of the most important elements of the game. One team succeeds in fooling the other with a certain play only until the opposing side devises a successful counterstrategy. The first team then makes use of the counterstrategy to launch a different attack. Thus, offensive and defensive maneuvers are constantly in flux, and the initial play, fake or formation is used only as a point of departure from which many successful plays may be improvised.

Basketball has similarities, too. Here the two tallest members of a team are matched against each other in the center position; the quickest guard is assigned to the most prolific opposing forward. By such a philosophy, the team concentrates its strength against opposing strength, doing what it can to compensate for any weaknesses.

In both sports, a great deal of precontest preparation goes into evaluating the opponent. Judo is—or should be—much the same.

Tsutomu Ohshima, a famous karate instructor, explained it this way: "There are three kinds of men in this world. The first is an idiot; he makes a mistake, makes the same mistake the very next day and continues to make that same mistake thereafter. The second type is the average man, who makes a mistake, sees it and corrects it. The third type is a genius, for he has been watching the mistakes of others and says to himself, 'I'm not going to make that mistake.' " Each of us, depending on the situation, falls into one of these categories at one time or another. Strive to stay within the genius category as much as possible.

One must have the ability to take an overview to become a strategist. Some of the more essential qualities that go into the makeup of a strategist are an awareness of one's own abilities and

weaknesses; an appreciation of the opponent's abilities and limitations; the knack for capitalizing on the vulnerabilities of an adversary; the flexibility to adapt to an opponent's changing attack, and perhaps most importantly, the will to win, an aggressive psychological attitude.

To find out about an opponent's physical condition, his strong and weak points, ask other competitors who have contended against him. Among the questions most commonly heard at tournaments are "What are his favorite techniques? Is he strong? Does he use right side, left side or both? Does he have good techniques on mat work?" Still, such an approach does not answer the need for training and preparation time. It would be better to study an opponent through films, videotapes or through the study of evaluation sheets like the one that follows.

┌─ COMPETITOR EVALUATION ─────────────────────┐

    Submitted by: _____
    Occasion: _____
    Date: _____

A.) Name: _____ Age: _____ Rank: _____
    Representing: _____
B.) Height: _____ Weight: _____
C.) Body Type (Circle) Muscular, Medium, Thin, Fat, etc. _____
    _____

D.) Strong Points: (Describe)
    1.) Physical Strengths: _____
        _____
        _____
    2.) Mental Attitude: _____
        _____
        _____
    3.) Emotional Attitude: _____
        _____
        _____
    4.) Skill Level (A. B. C. D. E.) List Techniques in order of effectiveness:
        Right Side _____   _____   _____   _____
        Left Side _____   _____   _____   _____
        Mat Evaluation: _____
        _____
        _____
        _____
        _____
        _____
    5.) Opponent's Strong Points: _____
        _____
        _____
    6.) Weak Points: _____
        _____
    7.) What is needed in order to win on your part (Explain). A) Physical
        Power, B) Mental Power, C) Emotional Stability, D) Skill, E) More
        Practice, F) More Tourney Experience, etc. _____
        _____
    8.) Use other side for additional comments or suggestions.

└───┘

UNITED STATES NATIONAL JUDO CHAMPIONS

Year	130 lb.	150 lb.	160 lb.	180 lb.	200 lb.	Heavyweight	Open Division	Grand Champion
1953	HATAE	NAKASHIMA		KIKUCHI		HUNT		HUNT
1954	SAKAKI	YAMADA		TAMURA		LEBELL		LEBELL
1955	TAKAHASI	YAMADA		OSAKO		LEBELL		LEBELL
1956	NOZAKI	EMI		TAMURA		OSAKO		OSAKO
1957	KUMAMOTO	OISHI		KATO		HARRIS		HARRIS
1958	NOZAKI	CHANKO		OSAKO		HARRIS		HARRIS
1959	NOZAKI	YOSHIOKA		TAMURA		WILLIAMS		WILLIAMS
1960		NOZAKI	SEINO	IMAMURA		HARRIS		IMAMURA
1961		NOZAKI	SEINO	CAMPBELL		HARRIS		HARRIS
1962		YOSHIDA	SHINOHARA	IMAMURA		CAMPBELL		SHINOHARA
1963		SEINO		SHINOHARA		OBAYASHI	CAMPBELL	SHINOHARA
	135 lb.		**165 lb.**					
1964	KOGA	SHIBATA	BREGMAN	H. KIMURA	K. UEMURA	G. UEMURA		G. UEMURA
1965	KOGA	SEINO	NISHIOKA	TOMODA	OBAYASHI		WALTERS	NISHIOKA
	139 lb.	**154 lb.**	**176 lb.**		**205 lb. Under**	**205 lb. Over**	**Open**	
1966	KOGA	MARUYAMA	NISHIOKA		EGUCHI	COAGE	BELMONT	EGUCHI
1967	KOGA	ARIMA	NAGATOSHI		NELSON	FISH	MAURO	NAGATOSHI
1968	KOGA	HIRAOKA	YAMASHITA		WATANABE	COAGE	ITOH	WATANABE
1969	OISHI	HIRAOKA	YAMASHITA		ICHINOE	COAGE	NOGUCHI	NOGUCHI
1970	FUKUHARA	MARUYAMA	NISHIOKA		HAAS	COAGE	KOBAYASHI	
1971	PARR	BURRIS	I. COHEN		NELSON	CARNERIO	SUKIMOTO	NELSON
1972	YAKATA	BURRIS	I. COHEN		GRAHAM	NELSON	WATTS	GRAHAM
1973	PRUZENSKY	BURRIS	SANFORD		SUKIMOTO	SEDGWICK	PERSON	SUKIMOTO
1974	MARTIN	BURRIS	I. COHEN		S. COHEN	ANDERSON	WOOLEY	I. COHEN
1975	NAKASONE	MARUYAMA	S. COHEN		MARTIN	COAGE	DAVIS	MARTIN
1976	COZZI	BURRIS	JOHNSTON-ONO		I. COHEN		WOOLEY	BURRIS
	132 lb.	**143 lb.**	**156 lb.**	**172 lb.**	**189 lb.**	**Under 209 lb.**	**Over 209 lb.**	**Open**
1977	NAKASONE	MARTIN	VINCENTI	S. COHEN	I. COHEN	WHITE	GIBBONS	OTAKA
1978	NAKASONE	MARTIN	SECK	JOHNSTON-ONO	WORTHAN	I. COHEN	SEDGWICK	SAYLOR
1979	NAKASONE	MARTIN	SECK	BARRON	WHITE	TUDELA	MITCHELL	GIBBONS
1980	DE LA TORRIENTE	GLOCK	SECK	BARRON	T. MARTIN	TUDELA	SAYLOR	MITCHELL
1981	CONDERAGES	MARTIN	SWAIN	YONEZUKA	BERLAND	WHITE	NELSON	SANTA MARIA
1982	CONDERAGES	MARTIN	SWAIN	BARRON	BERLAND	WHITE	NELSON	SANTA MARIA

PRACTICAL EXPERIENCE

Using your closest rival in judo, make out an evaluation sheet comparable to the preceding one. On the back side, list the ways and means you would use, based on the evaluation, to defeat him. If possible, give the plan a try at the next free practice session.

TEST YOURSELF

1. Discuss the most important items you, as a competitor, need note when entering in practice or competition.
2. Briefly describe the types of persons whom Ohshima-sensei (teacher) talks of.
3. Discuss the two methods most readily available in recording data on a potential opponent.
4. Cite three examples of key points you would look for in an opponent. Describe how you would plan to counteract his moves.

True-False Questions

1. The only strategy needed in judo is to attack or defend constantly.
2. Scouting an opponent is bad because it will scare you when you have to compete against him.
3. Strengths and weaknesses should be studied in scouting an opponent.
4. You must know your own abilities and limitations to plan your strategy.

Chapter VII

WHAT IT TAKES TO BE A CHAMP

WHAT IS ADVANCED STRATEGY LIKE IN JUDO?

Advanced strategy is found in the spirit in which it is practiced, rather than the techniques used. Although judo in the United States is not a competitive sport, a devotee will be nonetheless interested in the means used to win. Certain guidelines should be followed in order to become a top-grade competitor, and many of the ingredient qualities of a winner are a combination of physical and psychological factors.

It has often been said that on any one given day there is only a minute difference in the skill levels among the top four competitors of a weight class in a country. But where psychological factors are involved, an evaluation of these top competitors becomes a toss-up.

In 1961, the judo world came to a shattering realization that Japan could be beaten at its own game. Anton Geesink of Holland, in a spectacular and historic match, defeated Koji Sone of Japan and captured the coveted title of World Judo Champion. While none of the judo experts in the world could visualize a non-Japanese judo champion, Anton Geesink did, and he made a reality of his dream of winning.

How did Geesink become the world's undisputed champion in judo, a sport considered to be dominated by the Japanese alone? Ability plus the necessary psychological drive. How does one become a champion and what distinguishes him from the average, run-of-the-mill judo player? There are countless stories of champions who have had their dreams of championship come true.

Regardless of the motivations that quickened their hopes, as one of the songs from the musical, *South Pacific*, stated, "You gotta have a dream. If you don't have a dream, how ya gonna make a dream come true?"

PERSEVERANCE TO LEARN

Sayings such as, "Quitters never win and winners never quit," or "When the going gets tough, the tough get going," can be found in many gyms and dojos around the United States. They are hung there to remind the competitor that it takes hard work, guts and determination to succeed in competition. In learning, the importance of the quantity of judo knowledge acquired decreases near the top where the skills already learned are refined and honed to expertise. Enroute from nothing to something, the student discovers many plateaus, and, in striving to improve, it becomes increasingly harder for him to progress as he nears the top. Many expert competitors complain of being in a slump or feeling that they will not be able to improve beyond a level attained immediately prior to competition time. Those who progress at a steady pace, as opposed to those who practice judo in fits and spurts, seem to have the most success.

Ben Campbell and the 1964
Olympic team.

PROGRESS CHART: When learning new motor skills, the progress of most
individuals is hampered by periods of nonprogress (plateaus or slumps). In the
beginning stages of learning, these plateaus are relatively short and one quickly acquires added skill. As one continues with practice, however, progress
becomes slower and the plateaus become longer. The following graph, divided
into increments of time and progress, shows how different individuals react to
these plateaus and how their progress is affected.

A
• • • • • •

This person demonstrates good potential and at the beginning quickly pro-
gresses in gaining skill. But as progress becomes slower and more difficult
with longer pleateaus, he becomes discouraged and quits the activity alto-
gether.

B
_____

This person also makes rapid progress at the beginning, and like the first
person, he quits when it becomes more difficult. However, he later renews his
interest and continues to improve his skill but never supercedes Mr. C, who
started with less skill and slower improvement.

C
_ _ _ _

Although his initial progress is slower than the other two, this person is a
plodder who keeps going when faced with obstacles, thereby eventually gaining the greatest amount of skill. A person with innate potential as well as
perseverance has the makings of a champion.

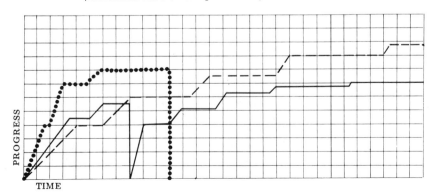

PROGRESS

TIME

Many potential champions cower before obstacles they feel are insurmountable; yet there are those able to meet and overcome even greater obstacles. Stories of such persons are plentiful, but one is especially noteworthy. Despite many setbacks and slumps, Ben Campbell showed the perseverance that made him a champion. The late 1950s saw him drop several matches to George Harris, three-time AAU judo grand champion. Defeating Harris became such an obsession with Campbell that he went to Japan to train.

There he found himself a lamb in a den of man-eating lions. Every day he forced himself to go to practice at Meiji University, and following each session, he was the worse for it. The practice at Meiji University for a judoka at that time, at least, stopped only when the student was unable to stand. Many times Campbell wondered if he would come out of judo practice in one piece. Each opponent who went against him tried his utmost literally to destroy him. Such practice sessions would be difficult to conceive of here in the United States, would be considered, in fact, mayhem. In Japan at that time, almost every workout left one with various injuries—whether a chafed neck from the judo gi, a cauliflower ear, bruised shins, sprained joints or just the simple contusions and bruises from being thrown.

This rigorous training requires a special perseverance. One of the few men in United States judo to have withstood its rigors is the exceptional Ben Campbell of Sacramento, California, who, at retirement, was a three-time National Champion, a Pan-American Gold Medalist and an Olympian.

LOSING IS BEING KILLED

There is something in the makeup of a champion that causes him to have an intense hatred of losing. Desmond Morris in his book *The Naked Ape* speculates that this hatred stems from a time when men had to fight physically to protect what was theirs—worldly possessions, mates, offspring and ideals. According to Morris, the athletic events of today are a throwback simulation of those ancient battles. To a champion, mock combat is not merely a matter of winning or losing a game but a subconscious struggle for survival. Thus, defeated, some champions consider a loss almost the same as death. The phrase "death of a champion" has been used time and again to convey the dismal defeat and mental collapse of a defeated champion.

To defend themselves from losing mock battles, many champions have devised specific psychological conditioning techniques. Among the most common is that of the so-called killer instinct that is so visible in most contact sports. Such athletes will themselves into hating an opponent—for even the slightest little fault. The way an opponent walks, his choice of clothes, a negative story or mannerism can be keyed on and used to build up a feeling of hatred in the hope that such a feeling of animosity will fuel the killer instinct and bring about a heightened desire for victory.

THE FEARLESSNESS OF NO FEAR

Just prior to the close of World War II, the Japanese brought into play a special, sacrificial tactic. *Kamikaze* pilots sacrificed their lives for a patriotic cause, that of winning for their losing nation. With almost the same zeal an athlete can commit himself mentally, emotionally and physically to winning, even when the contest may result in his death. That kind of a psyched-up person is most difficult to contend with, for he will go down fighting every bit of the way as a great athlete. In whatever form it may manifest itself, the quality of fearlessness is one of the most important factors in the makeup of a champion.

Suzuki Daisetsu, in his book *Zen and Japanese Culture*, tells the story of a tea man and a ruffian. At the insistence of Lord Yamanouchi of Tosa Province, a reluctant tea master was taken to Yedo (now Tokyo) on an official trip and was attired in a samurai's

Miyamoto Musashi

garment with two swords. While taking a stroll by himself in Yedo, the tea master was challenged by a ruffian—the very thing he feared would happen. The tea master was at first unable to speak but finally admitted that he was not really a samurai. The ruffian (a masterless samurai or ronin), discovering that his opponent was merely a tea master, replied that it would be an insult to the tea man's province if he did not defend its honor, although in actuality the ronin wanted only to take the tea master's money. The tea master replied, "If you so insist, we will try out our skills, but first I must finish my master's errand. Then I will return."

The ronin agreed and the tea master rushed to talk with the master of a fencing school, asking how he might die in the manner befitting a samurai. The swordsman, taken aback by the question, said, "You are unique. Most of my students come to ask me how to use a sword. You come to me and ask how to die. Before I teach you the art of dying, please serve me a cup of tea." Forgetting about the impending catastrophe, the tea master prepared tea as if there were nothing else in the world that mattered except serving the tea.

Deeply moved by the tea master's intense but natural concentration, the swordsman exclaimed, "That's it! That very state of mind is what you need tomorrow when you meet the ruffian. First, think you are going to serve tea for a guest and act accordingly. Draw your sword and close your eyes. When you hear a yell, strike him with your sword. It will probably end in a mutual slaying."

The tea master thanked the swordsman and went on to meet the ruffian. Following the swordsman's advice to the letter, the tea master boldly stood before his opponent. The opponent, who had previously seen before him a very different man, was now confronted by a man who was the embodiment of bravery. Instead of advancing, the ruffian retreated, cowed with the fear inspired by the superior concentration of his adversary.

DETERMINATION IS GRUELLING PRACTICE

In any instance, determination plays an important part in the psychological makeup of an athlete. If an athlete can't say, "I'll show them," he is many times lost.

Paul Maruyama, a 1970 National Judo Champion and one of America's top lightweight judoists, was once told by an official that he had only a high school level of proficiency in judo. He was also told that he had some psychological hangups about winning in international competition—especially against Japanese fighters. Determined to prove this official wrong, Paul worked out twice as hard as anyone around him. Wrapped in tape and despite his injuries and pain, he continued his practice, winning the Grand Championship for Southern California, the Air Force and the Collegiate Judo Nationals. This "small giant" still works out at least four times a week in Japan and is, to this day, determined and persevering.

Isao Inokuma, after becoming, at age 19, the youngest man ever to win the All-Japan Championships, had an unfortunate accident. When an operation on his once powerful back became necessary, doctors predicted he would never be able to compete as successfully as before. Following surgery, Inokuma came back undaunted to judo. Little by little, the *kama* (bear) showed signs of recovering both ability and title. He won the All-Japan Judo Championships twice. In 1964, he was an Olympics winner, and in 1965, won the World Championship.

Judo proficiency can be discussed in three basic categories: the beginner says to himself, "Now I am going to attack," and, so saying, may have already lost his chance; the intermediate says, "I am attacking now," but the advanced practitioner says, "I have attacked my opponent. How did I do that?" If the advanced judoka stops to think consciously of every movement, he regresses.

In one tournament, Tsutomu Ohshima lost himself. In the All-Japan Karate Championships of 1952, he was fighting for the championship title. Ohshima attacked and was met with a solid kick to the groin. "I somehow knew that the pain would not set in right away," he explained. "I said to myself, 'I might lose. I can't lose.' I didn't care if I died, but I had to win. Also, I was very

Isao Inokuma (Japan) dumping Kidnadz of USSR

angry that my opponent had no control over his kick. All these thoughts and feelings ran through my head at once. Before I knew what had happened, I found I had knocked out my opponent and won the first All-Japan Karate Championship."

Whether it comes about through a mastery of technique that has become automatic, or whether it is brought about from be-

Koichi Tohei, aikido master

coming angry with one's self or one's opponent, losing the self through concentration may be deliberate and controlled, or wholly spontaneous. But losing one's self is definitely a characteristic of a champion. Emotions supercede reason. The Japanese call this "*muga no kyochi*" or, as Suzuki explains it, "a state of mind of no mind."

CONCENTRATION OF EFFORT

Whether practicing or contesting, the judoist must focus all his attention on the task at hand. Nothing should enter his mind but the automatic impulses of attack and defense. While engaged in a contest, one judoist thought about his sweetheart. The next thing, he found himself on his back. Failing to devote all his concentration to the conflict, he was, in the literal sense of the phrase, swept off his feet.

Suzuki Daisetsu calls this ability to think of only one thing "prajna immovable." Prajna immovable is the virtue of single-minded concentration and devotion to exactly what one is doing. One should not be aware of others around him. In Western philosophy we try to fill our minds in order to know something; in Eastern philosophy, the idea is to empty the mind in order to know something. But the apparent contradiction in these concepts is one of semantics, for by either standard, concentration means to lose yourself in the activity, not to be conscious of time or space but to be totally committed.

CAN YOU DEFEAT YOURSELF?

When you enter a tournament and lose, who do you blame? When you get thrown or hit in practice, who do you blame? When you just can't enter into a technique or get into the groove of things, who do you blame? Proficient competitors usually know who to blame—themselves! It is primarily persons of less skill who blame the referees or opponents. An accomplished judoka will use a little introspection. In a well-adjusted judoist, the frustration and anger arising from not being able to defeat an opponent is most frequently directed at himself.

The competitor must train himself so that when a small voice inside says, "I'm tired, it's time to quit. I can't take anymore," it

is answered by, "Yes, I can. I will keep going." This means one must keep working even when tired, despite the fact that everything in the body cries out for rest. One must fight the impulse to quit—avoid capitulation as if it were a matter of life and death.

There is no substitute in any athletic or martial arts endeavor for good, hard practice sessions. Tough practice will build physically and add to the psychological makeup of the superior athlete. An athlete who has trained hard and gone through the tortures of rigorous training in preparation for a big tournament or match is less likely to give up mentally.

Yoshimi Osawa, who weighed 145 pounds, competed against some of the top men of his time. Although a slightly built person, he was able to topple many men larger than himself. One of the reasons for his ability to win was that he practiced twice as hard as his opponents. Many competitors of his time reported instances

where he would work out until perspiration soaked through the outer layer of his black belt. His face, after practice, would be flushed red, and from a slight distance one could even see vapors of his body heat rising into the air. When he had cooled down, little white patches of salt crystals were visible around his mouth where the perspiration had evaporated. It is not likely that Mr. Osawa would let all his hard practice go to waste by losing. By now a seventh dan, he is also an instructor for the special students at the Kodokan.

We might do well to compare this situation with poker. The more chips into the pot, the more a person wants to win and hates to lose. The more we practice, the more intense our desire to win.

War is a matter of life and death. When in the heat of battle, one must give his all to the task at hand. As in war, he must give no quarter and expect none. No foe is to be underestimated, and the only good foe is a defeated one. Remember, competition is a simulation of wars and battles.

PRACTICAL EXPERIENCE

On a sheet of paper, list the headings found in this section, leaving some space between each heading. Place your name under the heading that you feel most applies to your situation. Next, place the names of others in your class in appropriate categories. Study the positive and negative aspects of the attitudes under each category and attempt to plan your next contest strategy, either in the dojo or in a tournament, so it will be consistent with these psychological guidelines.

TEST YOURSELF

1. Explain the theory behind the success of the tea master as a samurai.
2. Under which category do you think Anton Geesink would be listed?
3. Are there any outstanding examples in your dojo of any of these psychological feats?
4. Which psychological ideal appeals to you? Why?

True-False Questions

1. A competitor's mental attitude is very important if he is to be a winner.
2. Just because a person believes he cannot be a champion doesn't mean he will not be a champion.
3. Determination and proficiency will help the competitor achieve his goals.

Chapter XIII

RANKING IN JUDO

The ranking system in judo is designed to test a student's degree of competence, knowledge of sport judo and to express his contribution to the sport of judo.

Traditionally, the levels of competency in the martial arts in feudal Japan were divided into four main categories: *oku-iri*, warrior; *moku-roku*, seasoned teacher; *menkyo*, highly seasoned and skilled warrior, and *kaidan*, or master technician.

Later, Dr. Kano, seeing a need for a more specific hierarchy, devised the *kyu-dan* system. Similar to the four categories of the feudal warriors system, Dr. Kano's innovation was soon adopted by many of the other modern martial arts. Basically, the *kyu* or *mudansha* were those who were not black belts and the *dan* or *yudansha* were those of black belt rank or higher.

The *kyu* system included grades of sixth *kyu* through first *kyu* —first *kyu* being the highest and sixth the lowest. Traditionally, sixth *kyu* through fourth *kyu* wore white belts. Through the use of the more recent European grading system, belt colors have been changed to include yellow, orange, blue, purple and green belts.

From third *kyu* to first *kyu*, the adult practitioner wears a brown belt to signify that he is no longer a beginner, and that he can display a degree of competency over most other white belts as far as knowledge of techniques, etiquette and history are concerned.

After first *kyu*, the order of degrees is reversed. First-degree black becomes the lowest in a scale that climbs all the way to 10th-degree black belt. Within the 10 black belt levels, there are

BELT COLORS

Rank	12 and under (Yonen rank)	13 to 17 (shonen rank)	17 and over (seinen rank)
6th Kyu (*Rokkyu*)	white	white	white
5th Kyu (*Gokyu*)	yellow	yellow	white
4th Kyu (*Yonkyu*)	orange	orange	green
3rd Kyu (*Sankyu*)	green	green	brown
2nd Kyu (*Nikyu*)	blue	blue	brown
1st Kyu (*Ikkyu*)	purple	purple	brown
1st Dan (*Shodan*)	none	black	black
2nd Dan (*Nidan*)	none	black	black
3rd Dan (*Sandan*)	none	black	black
4th Dan (*Yodan*)	none	black	black
5th Dan (*Godan*)	none	black	black
6th Dan (*Rokudan*)	none	black	red and white
7th Dan (*Shichidan*)	none	black	red and white
8th Dan (*Hachidan*)	none	black	red and white
9th Dan (*Kudan*)	none	black	red
10th Dan (*Judan*)	none	black	red

certain levels at which one is permitted to wear a different colored belt to show a higher degree of competency.

Between first and fifth degrees, one is only permitted to wear a black belt. Between sixth and eighth *dan*, the bearer may wear either a black or red-and-white belt. Ninth and 10th degrees were allowed to wear an all-red belt. To date, there have been seven 10th-degree black belts. There are no further plans to bestow any more.

Seated are all but one of the 10th-degrees; from left to right: Shotaro Tabata, Kunisaburo Iizuka, Hidekazu Nagaoka, Dr. Jogoro Kano, Yoshiaki Yamashita, Kaichiro Samura, Kyuzo Mifune. Standing in middle is Roy "Pop" Moore Sr. (5th dan). To his left, Professor Yamauchi, 8th dan, pioneer in American judo, along with Seigo Murakami, 8th dan. The only 10th-degree not in the photo is Hajime Isogai, who was probably in the Southern portion of Japan at the time.

Ranks are bestowed by the individual countries except where the countries voluntarily receive their rank from the mecca of judo, the Kodokan. Most countries are affiliated with either the Kodokan directly or with the International Judo Federation,

Kano, seated with great jujitsu masters and students

whose rank regulations differ only slightly from those of the Kodokan.

Each member nation of IJF in turn is sanctioned to bestow upon a *yudan-shakai* or black belt association the power to promote its members in accordance with the limitations placed on its authority to promote.

Ranks are usually given on the basis of how well one does in tournament play, or what one has done to further the sport. Other considerations may include character, age, time in grade, contest record, kata or forms proficiency, teaching ability, clinics given, coaching ability, officiating and administrative ability.

As a rule, tournament players receive their rank for tournaments up to as high as fifth degree. Anything from sixth degree on up is usually honorary in nature, and the tougher competitors are usually found among the second through fourth-degree ranks.

In recent years, there has been a certain preoccupation with judo degrees in that most people go to great lengths to receive the next-higher rank when it should be remembered that, as Don Draeger, a famous martial artist and fellow judoman, once wrote —and this should be imprinted in our minds—"Rank follows the man" not "Man follows the rank."

With the award of a black belt goes a certain amount of power, prestige, integrity and a level of proven competency. But the idea that the attainment of a black belt is the ultimate achievement of a martial artist is an illusion—as anyone really familiar with the martial arts will tell you.

As in the West, where the holder of a gun had a certain amount of respect, so it is with the black belt holder. What was done with it, and how a man established his reputation, however, made a big difference. The same is true in judo today.

The only way to truly advance is through hard work and dedication.

PRACTICAL EXPERIENCE

Politely ask some high-ranking black belt how far a black belt can ordinarily advance through competition.

TEST YOURSELF

1. Give the names of the four categories of attainment in feudal Japan.
2. Explain what is meant by *mudansha* and *yudansha* and how they tie in with the *kyu-dan* system of grading.
3. Name the main belt colors used in judo.
4. Give the three belt colors with the *dan* system and the levels at which they are worn.
5. Give the names of the two main sources of rank.
6. Explain how one may advance in judo.

True-False Questions

1. *Shodan* is the highest-ranking black belt.
2. *Kyu* designates the competitor as a brown belt.
3. There have been over one hundred 10th-degree black belts.
4. Nineteen Americans have earned their 10th-degree black belts.
5. Competitors may earn up to sixth-degree black belts.
6. *Dan* signifies the competitor as a black belt.
7. Between sixth and eighth-degree black belts, the bearer may wear a red-and-white belt.
8. Various areas in the United States may promote competitors to different levels.
9. Rank follows the man, not man following the rank.
10. The three main color ranks are green, brown and black.

Chapter IX

AUXILIARY TRAINING METHODS

ARE THERE OTHER METHODS OF TRAINING FOR JUDO?

Naturally, persons wanting better technical proficiency in judo will have to work diligently at training themselves to that end. Participants uninterested in the competitive aspect of the sport may yet enjoy the challenge of practicing with persons of equal or better skill levels. The person who does judo strictly for recreational purposes may limit himself to light *randori* or free practice.

For the competitive participant, the road to success is much more difficult. He must physically train himself in many ways, including anaerobic as well as aerobic methods. Weight training and running or endurance-type exercises are a prerequisite. As will be amplified later in this concept, in addition to regular *randori* practice, the competitor must engage in extensive *uchikomi* and *sutegeiko.*

Because of the wide range of material available on weight training and running, only a few suggestions concerning these methods of training will be given as guidelines.

Running is an aerobic activity requiring a lot of oxygen. The person trained in aerobic activity is better prepared to cope with the trauma of "pooping out." Running increases the participant's capacities in the following ways: the heart puts out more blood per beat, thus cutting down the amount of beats required per minute; more oxygen is carried in the blood stream, allowing an increasing amount of oxygen to be passed from the blood to the

Chris Dolman

Isao Okano

muscle tissues (this decreases the lactic acid buildup—the major cause of sore, tired muscles), and a greater exchange of oxygen takes place between the blood stream and the lungs, with less carbon dioxide being given off.

When getting into shape aerobically, most major competitors run at least 15 minutes a day, at a moderate speed. Listed below are other means of realizing the benefits of aerobic exercising:

1. Interval running—on a regular, quarter-mile track, sprint the straightaways and walk the turns.
2. *Fartlek*-run, at random, over cross-country terrain, alternatively fast and slow.
3. Backward run—run backwards around a track.

PRACTICAL EXPERIENCE

Using the three methods of running suggested, record the distance run and the time required. Keep a record of this over a period of three months and see if there is an increase in amount of work done for that period of time spent. Also check your pulse at the beginning, middle and end of the three-month period to see if its rate has decreased.

Weight training is an anaerobic strength activity. The rule of thumb in weight lifting is that bulk or large muscles are a result of extremely heavy weights with few repetitions. Definition and muscular strength are achieved through the use of lesser weight but increased repetitions. An easy method of determining when to rest is to feel if the muscles are warm or fatigued. If progress is to be gained, however, it is important to work in an overload situation, pushing yourself beyond normal limitations without causing injury. This is called the overload method of training.

PRACTICAL EXPERIENCE

Using a set of weights which you feel you can handle, go through the overload method of weight training. Continue this over a three-month period and see if you can feel an increase in muscular strength and endurance.

IMPROVEMENT IN JUDO SKILLS IS ACCOMPLISHED THROUGH TWO AUXILIARY EXERCISES— UCHIKOMI AND SUTEGEIKO

The two fundamental training methods employed in increasing judo skills are *uchikomi* (nonthrowing attack) and *sutegeiko* (non-resistive throwing) drills.

Uchikomi Drills

Uchikomi's repetitious, nonthrowing attack drills are one of the finest ways in which to learn a technique. Almost every major competitor throughout the world uses *uchikomi* to improve his technique. A competitor practicing *uchikomi* will probably do one of two kinds—static or dynamic.

In static *uchikomi*, one man stands erect while the other goes into position for the throw. He does this continuously without throwing his partner, who, on the other hand, offers partial resistance to the attacker's entry.

In dynamic *uchikomi*, both the attacker and the defender move about in order to simulate an actual *randori*. The attacker again continuously enters and takes his partner up to the point where, if he were to go any further, he would throw him. The differences and the benefits of this type of practice lie in the fact that the opponent is moving, whereas in static *uchikomi* the opponent is standing still.

Whichever type of *uchikomi* is used, there are many benefits to be derived from the practice. *Uchikomi* refines and trains reflexes, strengthens muscles, promotes endurance, adds speed to your technique, perfects techniques, instills confidence and develops psychological vigor.

Trained Reflexes

Anything done over and over becomes second-nature. Likewise in judo. The ultimate in trained reflex occurs when, through your *uchikomi* drills, you one day find in practice that you've thrown your opponent and you have to stop and ask yourself how he got down there—and neither you nor he can remember.

Strengthens Muscles
In judo there is a saying that goes:

> *Kimura no mae wa Kimura nashi,*
> *Kimura no ato wa Kimura nashi.*

This, when translated, means, "Before Kimura there was no Kimura; after Kimura there is no Kimura." The man referred to is Masahiko Kimura, perhaps the strongest judoman ever produced. He won championship after championship with his famous one-arm shoulder throw, *ippon seoinage*. Nine years in succession, he won what would be the equivalent of the All-Japan Championship today. There is no record of his ever losing a judo match.

One of the main ways in which he would practice was by performing *uchikomi* on a tree! He would wrap his *obi* (belt) around a trunk and proceed to try to pull the tree out of the ground— roots, limbs, branches and all. He did so many vigorous *uchikomi* on the tree that his back turned raw and bled. Where once an erect tree stood, afterwards stood a crooked one. Even the ground around the tree had been altered by his heavy, scuffling feet. After some time on his regimen of tree *uchikomi*, he found it easy to throw humans—they didn't have roots to hold them down. This practice strengthened his hips and legs. In the Western world, this could be called isometric exercise.

Endurance
Wind, stamina and endurance increase the capacity to withstand fatigue.

Uchikomi can be used to develop wind. In Japan, it is not uncommon to see college judoka do one or two hundred *uchikomi* nonstop. When standing close to them and listening to their breathing, it is not very hard to realize that it builds stamina and perfection. Some enthusiastic judoka have tried to see how many they can do perfectly without stopping, even passing the five hundred mark.

Speed

Kazuo Shinohara, twice United States Grand Champion, had the ability to throw an opponent so fast that he could, at times, leave the opponent unconscious upon impact with the mat. He relates, "*Uchikomi* practice is one of the best methods in building a strong, fast throw. Through the practice of *uchikomi*, it was possible for me to cut down the amount of time that it took to enter into a technique."

When Shinohara first started doing his *uchikomi*, he could only do a few in one minute. Later, through constant practice, he accelerated his rate until he could go into his technique in less than a second per try. In speeding up his ability, he achieved two things. He left less time for his opponent to give him resistance and he added more momentum to his throw.

With practice, anyone can build up to 60 *uchikomi* per minute or one entry per second. These *uchikomi* must be done in perfect form in order to be effective for competition. Anyone can do 60 *uchikomi* in a sloppy manner, but very few will take the effort to perfect their own techniques.

Confidence

Self-confidence is a state of mind characterized by a person's reliance on himself or his circumstances. To add to this definition, we might say that this confidence is also a product of one's previous experience.

Through practice of *uchikomi*, if a person can enter into a waza (technique) in a split-second, if a person can do *uchikomi* on a tree and shake its leaves off, if a person can perform two hundred *uchikomi* at one time without stopping to rest, if a judoka can do his *uchikomi* until he is even going through them in his sleep, then it can be said that *uchikomi* will add to the confidence of any serious judoka's ability to perform that technique quickly and expertly in the future.

PRACTICAL EXPERIENCE

With a partner, choose one of the basic techniques in Chapter III and practice entering into the technique continuously 30 times. Make sure the technique is applied correctly. Then try to speed up the number of entries per minute until you can do at least 40 per minute correctly.

Throwing Exercise (Sutegeiko)

As a method of practice, the nonresistant throwing exercise (*sutegeiko*) plays the greatest part in enabling the student to experience and learn a technique. *Sutegeiko* is accomplished by having the thrower throw the receiver with little or no resistance from the receiver. At each execution of the technique, the thrower should try to correct his own mistakes. There are no definite rules as to the speed with which the technique should be applied. It can only be suggested here that continuous progression should be from slow to fast with emphasis always on correct form.

Types of Sutegeiko

Sutegeiko practice methods, like *uchikomi* drills, are broken up into two categories—static and dynamic. In static *sutegeiko*, both parties exchange throws, one for one, five for five, from a still position. Regardless of the number per turn, the throws should all be of the same type for both partners; that is, if footsweeps are used, they should be practiced exclusively throughout the set.

Dynamic *sutegeiko* means that both parties are in a moving situation, without being confined to a specific area. This freedom to move about and throw each other requires more skill than the static *sutegeiko*, since it obviously is easier to practice a skill against a still object than a moving target. Like *randori* or actual competition, dynamic *sutegeiko* affords the opportunity to adapt to a moving situation.

PRACTICAL EXPERIENCE

Using the same technique as in *uchikomi*, practice static then dynamic *sutegeiko*. Be sure to practice the attacks from all positions and directions in order to allow for the various body movements of future opponents.

TEST YOURSELF

1. List the four main ways to train for judo.
2. Give the scientific names for the equivalent of strength and endurance activities.
3. Discuss the physical benefits that can be found from an activity such as running.
4. List the three methods of running mentioned.
5. Discuss the rules of thumb of weight training.
6. Describe the overload method of weight training.
7. List the five areas that *uchikomi* practice enhances skill and give a brief discussion of each.
8. Describe how *uchikomi* is done.
9. Discuss the significance of the *sutegeiko* practice.
10. List the two types of *uchikomi* and *sutegeiko* drills.

True-False Questions

1. Running is an excellent training device for judo.
2. Weight lifting is not good for judoists because it bunches the muscles and makes the competitor slow.
3. *Uchikomi*, repetitions and nonthrowing attack drills are some of the best ways for a competitor to learn a technique.
4. *Sutegeiko* (nonresistive throwing) should be done in moderation so the competitor is not accidentally hurt.
5. *Uchikomi* refines and trains the reflexes while adding speed to the technique.
6. *Sutegeiko* perfects the technique of the competitor.
7. Endurance is only important if a competitor is on a national team where the matches are 10 minutes long.
8. *Uchikomi* and *sutegeiko* give a competitor confidence in his throwing ability.
9. Dynamic and static *uchikomi* are both important in developing a technique.
10. Dynamic *sutegeiko* means one opponent is moving while the other is stationary.

Chapter X

THE HISTORY OF JUDO
AND ITS DEVELOPMENT IN THE UNITED STATES

In his book, *On Aggression*, Konrad Lorenz suggests that some of the major historical instances of aggressive behavior involved the preservation of self, kin, terrority and species. Indeed, the history of aggression is antique. It is etched in the broken and scarred cranial specimens of paleolithic man and shown in paintings created 35,000 years ago on cave walls in Lascaux, France. Beni Hasan's Egyptian tomb paintings dating back to 3,400 B.C. depict many wrestling maneuvers, and our records of Fifth and Sixth Century B.C. depicting physical contests between such characters as Hercules and Antaeus can be found on Greek vases.

The story of judo can be linked to the ideas of preservation. The first recorded instance of a bare-handed competition in Japan, according to *The Illustrated Kodokan* book, dates back to 23 A.D. The event, called a *Chikara Kurabe*, translates into plain English as a strength-comparison match. Later attempts to develop a system of defenses and attacks led to what we know as jujitsu. During the feudal period of Japanese history, many jujitsu schools flourished. Notable among the various styles were *takenouchi-ryu, kito-ryu, jikishin-ryu, kyushin-ryu, yoshin-ryu, mirua-ryu, sekiguchi-ryu* and the *tenshin shinyo-ryu*.

Mr. G. Koizumi, in his astutely written book, *My Study of Judo*, is particularly effective when discussing the evolution of jujitsu and judo.

"As to the origin and native land of jujitsu, there are several opinions, but they are found to be mere assumptions based on narratives relating to the founding of certain schools, or some incidental records or illustrations found in the ancient manuscripts not only in Japan, but in China, Persia, Germany and Egypt. There is no record by which the origins of jujitsu can be definitely established. It would, however, be rational to assume that ever since the creation, with the instinct for self-preservation, man has had to fight for existence and was inspired to develop an art or skill to implement the body mechanism for this purpose. In such efforts, the development may have taken various courses according to the condition of life or tribal circumstance, but the object and mechanics of the body being common, the results could not have been so very different from each other. No doubt this is the reason for finding records relating to the practice of arts similar to jujitsu in various parts of the world, and also for the lack of records of its origins.

"However, there are sufficient records to prove that the arts known under the term of jujitsu were developed to the present standard of excellence in Japan during her feudal days (the 12th—19th centuries), by the warriors, or samurai. With the performance of their daily task, in the battlefield or in upholding law and order, it was of vital importance for the warriors to have a knowledge of and skill in jujitsu. Hence the competitive efforts for technical superiority and secrecy, such as are found today among nations in regard to armaments.

"As a policy of the feudalistic ruling, jujitsu was a monopolized training for the warriors, and those who found or acquired new methods kept them as family or school secrets, to be taught only to chosen pupils. In the early days the techniques must have been quite primitive, but during the period from the 16th to the 19th century, skillful masters appeared and founded schools, each with its own particular merits. These flourished until the feudal system came to an end in 1867.

"At the beginning of the new era of frantic national efforts to modernize and adopt the Western cultures, jujitsu was left to decay as a relic of the past. But waves of reaction against radical innovations brought jujitsu to the surface again. Its merits were reviewed, the police and naval authorities taking a special interest.

"At this juncture, judo made its appearance. At a specially

convened tournament on June 10th, 1886, at police headquarters, the judo system of training proved its superiority conclusively against that of jujitsu by scoring nine wins and one draw out of 10 contests. This event was the turning point for securing public recognition of judo and establishing it on a firm basis."

Teacher, professor, educator, sportsman, philosopher, humanitarian, politician and shihan—these were the titles earned in one lifetime by the founder of judo, Jigoro Kano. Judo originated in Japan, in the year 1882, when its founder, Jigoro Kano, at the age of 22, opened his first practice hall, the Kodokan Judo Dojo.

At 18, he began a study of jujitsu. A year later, former United States President Grant visited Japan and witnessed a demonstration of jujitsu in which Jigoro Kano participated.

The first United States contact with true judo came in 1889, when Kano lectured on the educational value of judo before a group of foreign dignitaries. There were several Americans at the lecture, but their contact with judo was very slight and entirely of an informational nature.

The first American to study seriously at the Kodokan was

Professor Ladd of Yale University, who came to the Kodokan in 1889. Kano taught Ladd judo theory and technique. The American also studied *nage, katame* and *atemi-waza*, besides being introduced to *koshiki no kata* by Kano.

Although the number of American visitors at the Kodokan did not rise immediately after Ladd's first incursion, Professor John Dewey of Columbia University later went to the Kodokan to observe and receive an introduction to judo. Dewey discussed Kodokan judo with Kano and may have been instrumental in beginning one of the pioneer American programs in judo at Columbia.

Of judo, John Dewey wrote the following in his *Letters from China and Japan*, published by E.P. Dutton and Company, New York, 1920, and reprinted by Dennis Helm and Paul Armetta in *Judo U.S.A.*, July 1977:

"My other experience that I have not written about is seeing judo. The great judo expert is president of a normal school, and he arranged a special exhibition by experts for my benefit, he explaining the theory of each part of it in advance. It took place Sunday morning in a big judo hall, and there were lots of couples doing 'free' work too; they are too quick for my eye in that to see anything but persons suddenly thrown over somebody's back and flopped down on the ground. It is really an art. The Professor took the old practices and studied them, worked out their mechanical principles and then devised a graded scientific set of tricks, but it is based on the elementary laws of mechanics, a study of the equilibrium of the human body, the ways in which it is disturbed, how to recover your own and take advantage of the shiftings of the center of gravity of the other person. The first thing that is taught is how to fall down without being hurt, that alone is worth the price of admission and ought to be taught in all our gyms. It isn't a good substitute for out-of-doors games, but I think it is much better than most of our inside formal gymnastics. The mental element is much stronger. In short, I think a study ought to be made here from the standpoint of conscious control. . . . I noticed at the judo hall the small waists of all these people; they breathe all ways (sic) from the abdomen. Their biceps are not especially large, but their forearms are larger than any I have ever seen. I have yet to see a Japanese throw his back when he rises. In the army they have an indirect method of getting deep breathing which really goes back to the Buddhist Zen teaching of the old samurai. However, they have adopted a lot of the modern physical exercise from other armies."

Leon J. Garrie helped with research by contributing the following information:

On the 24th of July, 1905, representatives of the leading jujitsu schools (ryu) of Japan gathered at the Butokukai Institute in Kyoto to decide the forms of Kodokan judo and to continue the development of the technical forms of the sport. These schools were Sosuishiryu, Fusenryu, Sekiguchiryu, Takeuchiryu, Miuraryu, Kyushinryu and Yoshinryu. Of the above-listed ancient jujitsu schools, only Sosuishiryu and Sekiguchiryu remain traditional, and in accordance with Japanese government law, incorporate modern teachings of judo, aikido and modern jujitsu, preserving the ancient jujitsu techniques in kata forms only.

By 1908, the Kodokan had a total of 13 American members studying in Japan.

The Kodokan became an official foundation in May, 1909, and two years later, in April, 1911, the Kodokan Dan-Grade Holders (Black Belt) Association was organized and 10 years later was followed by the Judo Medical Research Society. When Jigoro Kano called judo "a way of human development understandable to people all over the world," he was already attempting to organize an International Judo Federation to spread interest in judo. By 1912, Jigoro Kano had made no fewer than nine trips abroad to create interest in the new Japanese sport. By this time, many foreigners, mostly sailors and merchant seamen, were training at the Kodokan. Books on judo in foreign languages were being printed. Thus, before the outbreak of World War I, dojos had been established in the United States, Britain, France, Canada and India, as well as in Russia, China and Korea.

Jigoro Kano's activities were not limited to judo alone but extended far beyond judo or gymnastics. Always interested in the advancement of physical activities, Jigoro Kano did much to import and spread modern Western sports throughout Japan. Today his country honors him as the "Father of modern sports and physical education."

In 1935, Jigoro Kano received the Asahi Prize for "outstanding contributions in the fields of art, science and sports." Three years later, he went to an International Olympic Council meeting in Cairo, where he succeeded in getting Tokyo nominated as the site of the 1940 Olympics. For the first time, judo was to be included as one of the events. It turned out to be the shihan's crowning achievement, but the cataclysm of World War II was to force its Olympic introduction to be postponed for another 25 years. On his way home from that momentous conference on board the SS Hikawa Maru on the 4th of May, 1938, Jigoro Kano died from pneumonia at the age of 78 years.

The Kodokan Judo Institute has changed its location many times since it was originally founded. In 1919, it occupied a two-story, 514-mat-area main dojo in the Suidobashi area. In 1958, the new seven-story building at 20-2 Kasugo cho, Bunkyo Ku, in Tokyo, was completed and named the "International Headquarters of Judo." Today, a tall, bronze statue of the founder, Jigoro Kano, stands before the main entrance hall.

By 1952, when there were over 66 nations throughout the world playing judo, the International Judo Federation (IJF) was founded, with Risei Kano, son of the originator of judo, as its first president. The Kodokan Judo Institute became revered as the world headquarters of judo, and for the very first time, judo was included in the Olympic Games, with Japan as the host nation in the 1964 Tokyo Olympiad. Thus, judo reached the top of the philosophical mountain of accomplishments for which its founder had so ardently wished.

Then began a period of decline. In 1965, President Kano was voted out as IJF international president, and Charles Palmer of England was elected, with P. Bonet Maury of France as secretary-general. The Kodokan still retains enormous prestige throughout the world, and President Kano adds to Kodokan influence throughout the world by acting as head of the All-Japan Judo Federation and the Judo Federation of Asia as well, of which the Kodokan Judo Institute is the headquarters. Kodokan Judo Institute is the sole grading authority in the whole of Japan. Many foreign students from all over the world travel to the Kodokan Judo Institute to study judo, take examinations and seek promotion to higher grades, because they continue to regard the birthplace of judo as the only authority of Japanese judo.

Now let's flash back to 1902, the beginning of judo in the United States. Yoshiaki Yamashita was the first man to teach judo in the United States. In 1902, on the invitation of Graham Hill, director of the Northern Railroad, Yamashita came to the United

States. He and his wife stayed in America for seven years, teaching at Harvard University, the Naval Academy and the White House. Yamashita's pioneering effort brought him many distinguished students, including Theodore Roosevelt, President of the United States. President Roosevelt's son also studied with Yamashita, as did the grandson of Robert E. Lee.

Mrs. Yamashita also taught judo. Her most notable student was Mrs. Wadsworth. The Yamashitas returned to Japan in 1909, and in 1932, Yoshiaki Yamashita was promoted to 10th dan.

Known as the first person to sign the rolls of the Kodokan, Shumeshiro Tomita came to the United States from Japan in 1903. Tomita also had the honor of competing in the match between Kodokan judo and jujitsu sponsored by the Tokyo Police Department. The tournament was instrumental in establishing Kodokan judo in Japan. Kodokan judo practitioners defeated seven of nine jujitsu opponents in the matches and tied the other two. Not only was Tomita instrumental in furthering judo in Japan, he was one of the first judo professors to teach in the United States. He stayed seven years and taught judo at Princeton and Columbia Universities.

After Tomita and Yamashita, many judo sensei came to the United States. Among the very first were Miada Kose, Sataki Nobushita and Takugoro Ito. Because of the large Japanese population, judo proliferated on the West Coast. Los Angeles, Seattle and San Francisco became major judo centers.

The early pioneers of judo in this country who developed judo in the larger Japanese communities were: Taguchi (7th dan), Yamauchi (6th dan), Sakata (6th dan), Kumagai (6th dan), Suzuki (5th dan), Koshima (5th dan), Matsuria (5th dan), Kuioi (5th dan) and Hiashi (5th dan).

As a result of Professor Kano's 1932 visit, four United States judo Yudanshakai (Black Belt Associations) were formed and became, in time, directly affiliated with the Kodokan in Tokyo, Japan. They were Southern California, Northern California, Seattle and Hawaii.

During the 1930s, the West Coast of the United States was about the only locale where judo was actively practiced—and that was principally in the Seattle, Washington, and Southern California areas. In Southern California, Professor Yamauchi was a pioneer in judo instruction, and during the mid-'30s initiated

24-man team contests between Southern California and Seattle. Los Angeles and Seattle had the strongest judo groups at that time. Tasuke Hagio was the captain of the Southern California team and Kaname Kumiyuki, known to most as Kenneth Kuniyuki, was captain of the Seattle team. The results were always close. Seattle won the *ippon-shobu* (point system) and lost to Los Angeles in *kohaku*. In the second contest, two years after the first, just the opposite took place.

Ironically, World War II had a beneficial influence on judo in that so many Japanese Americans were sent to detention camps, where the major pastime became the practice of judo. Therefore, out of those camps came a finely trained nucleus of judo teachers. Released from the camps, many chose not to return to the West Coast but settled and ultimately taught judo in other portions of the United States.

Currently, there are 23 judo associations within the framework of the United States Judo Association and numerous associations within the rival association, the United States Judo Federation. Each has a membership of approximately 20,000.

College judo, as was indicated previously, started with Professor Ladd, who introduced it to Columbia University about the turn of the century.

_____

PRACTICAL APPLICATION

Study other references listed in Chapter XII (Resources) and look for another historical view.

TEST YOURSELF

1. What is the earliest Japanese recorded date of barehanded competition?
2. When was judo first introduced to the United States?
3. What part did John Dewey have in developing United States judo?
4. What President studied judo?
5. What two associations exist in the United States today?

True-False Questions

1. Jigoro Kano originated judo in 1882 at the Kodokan Judo Dojo.
2. Professor Ladd was the first American to study at the Kodokan.
3. Kano was interested solely in the development of judo in Japan.
4. Judo was first introduced in the 1940 Tokyo Olympics and was a major success.
5. In 1965, Charles Palmer of England was voted president of the International Judo Federation.
6. Yamashita was the first man to teach judo in the United States, and one of his first pupils was Theodore Roosevelt.
7. *Yudanshakai* means Black Belt Associations that are affiliated with the Kodokan in Japan.
8. The West Coast has been a stronghold of judo since the 1930s, but recently other areas have developed outstanding judoists.
9. There are over 20 judo associations in the framework of the United States Judo Association.

Chapter XI

JUDO PHILOSOPHY,
A MEANS FOR THE ELEVATION OF LIFE

IS JUDO JUST ANOTHER SPORT?
WHAT IS THE PHILOSOPHY OF JUDO?

It is to be hoped that an understanding of the development and philosophy of judo will assist the beginner in developing a deep insight into the nature and spirit of judo.

The philosophy of judo, as originally explained by its founder, Jigoro Kano, has been unknown or misunderstood for too long in the Western world.

That judo has come a long way from its humble beginnings at the first Kodokan Judo Dojo, Jigoro Kano, were he alive today, would be quick to observe. On the other hand, if he could peer into today's modern practice of judo, his glance would, perhaps, be tinged with sadness and disappointment at the directions taken by many judoka. Much of the inner meaning he emphasized seems obscured, if not lost.

Somehow, through the passage of time, judo's true meaning has been diffused by its many practitioners. Its once far-reaching goals, which were of major importance for mankind's benefit, have been regrettably scrambled or obscured in translation. Perhaps too much was left to intuition, or perhaps, given the lack of literature available on basic judo philosophy, younger sensei never had sufficient opportunities to grasp the full meaning of judo.

For all practical purposes, Jigoro Kano's two maxims—"mutual welfare and benefit" and "maximum efficiency with minimum effort"—are about the extent of most judoka's understanding of the philosophy of judo. Various activities were made a part of the college curriculum, including gymnastics, European football (soccer), swimming, judo and Oriental fencing (kendo). Later, other activities were added to the curriculum, such as when G.H. Brown brought basketball to Japan.

Upon graduation, Kano's newly accredited teachers went out into the field and taught physical education along with the required academic subjects. Thus, Japan's first physical education program began to bloom, and along with it, the nation's health.

It is interesting to note that through his program, Dr. Kano achieved many firsts: mandatory physical education, incorporation of various physical activities into one program and the training of physical education teachers to service Japan's elementary and secondary education.

PHILOSOPHY OF PHYSICAL EDUCATION

To outline Dr. Jigoro Kano's philosophy of physical education, let us look at some of his statements concerning the three areas which he believed physical education helped to build.

"There are two types of judo—small judo and large judo," explains Dr. Kano. "Small judo is concerned only with techniques and the building of the body. Large judo is mindful of the pursuit of the purpose of life: the soul and the body used in the most effective manner for a good result."

KANO'S PHILOSOPHY OF JUDO

In view of the fact that the influence of jujitsu was waning, that its basis of bushido philosophy had become outmoded by modern times, it was refreshing to find that a young man of 22 was struggling to modernize the feudalistic jujitsu systems. To set it apart from jujitsu, which means "gentle art," Dr. Kano's method of self-defense was called judo, meaning the "gentle way." Where jujitsu was mainly concerned with techniques of overcoming an adversary, judo was concerned not only with self-defense techniques but the physical conditioning and total health that could be derived from its practice. Dr. Kano felt that if judo were practiced correctly, its results would be beneficial to all human beings.

(If physical activity is used only to build the body, it is called physical education; however, if physical activity is used for living, then it is considered a means for the elevation of life.)

Summed up in three short sentences are the basic maxims of Dr. Kano which convey his philosophy of his beloved judo: *"Jiko no kansei," "Jitta kyoe," "Seiryoku zenryo."*

The meaning of the first maxim, *jiko no kansei*, is to strive for perfection as a human being—but what is perfection? According to Dr. Kano, perfection could be found in an individual who had good health, intelligence, good character and the ability to know worth. As far as the individual within society is concerned, Dr. Kano believed that he should work toward attaining wealth (not always in terms of money), a capability and willingness to help the world, while cultivating trust and respect from and for others.

MUTUAL WELFARE AND BENEFIT

The literal meaning of the second maxim, *jitta kyoe*, is mutual welfare and benefit. This is an important principle, because it counterbalances the first maxim. If a person strives only for his own perfection, he will inevitably come in conflict with others. This is why the founder felt that even though we as individuals may strive for perfection, we must also consider those about us. This is basically the idea of give and take.

More and more, our world relies on this principle of mutual welfare and benefit. We can no longer live as hermits. In living with others, life becomes a joint effort, and we are all able to accomplish greater things than if we tried to live by ourselves. Even if we were to amass a fortune on our own, we would still find it necessary to deal with others. Whenever men have tried to horde everything to themselves, others became jealous and cheated, toppled or conquered them, whether as individuals, states or groups of nations.

"Needless to say," Kano continues, "there is a gap between Utopia and the sometimes-reality." As an example, the founder cites, "In the case of war, we cannot share with our enemies. We must side with and stick by our nation." The founder concludes, "Build yourself first, then help others. You have to think of yourself first in a positive sense of progress."

EFFICIENCY AND EFFORT

The third maxim, *seiryoku zenryo*, means maximum efficiency with minimum effort. To explain this, Dr. Kano related a story of a school friend who would always finish his studies before the young founder could. How was it, he wondered, that his friend should consistently finish before him when they both had the same amount of work? On top of that, his friend always seemed to do a better job than he did. This frustrating experience led Kano to study why his friend performed with more excellent results and less effort. As an explanation, the founder offered, "In order to study the maxim of *seiryoku zenryo*, we must first know what energy is. Energy is life-force or the force essential for living. The correct use of this energy will result in maximum efficiency with minimum effort."

Judo or the "gentle way" is a means whereby one can find out how to use energy more effectively. It was the founder's hope that once these principles were mastered in judo, they could be applied to everyday life.

If life were like a mountain, judo would be like climbing. First we must be strong enough to climb. The bigger the mountain, the more help will be needed from others. We must map our path and follow it through. The higher up the mountain we ascend, the more clearly we can see that there are other roads or ways to reach the top. The higher we climb, the more we are able to appreciate the struggle and accomplishments of others.

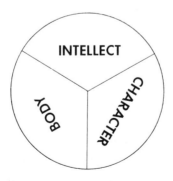

The Body: "The body is the instrument for the purpose of life, without which there is nothing." This statement clearly implies that one's health is of primary importance. It is self-evident that without the proper care of one's body, it will lose its efficiency, vitality and its reason for being.

Character: "Because we are alive in this world as humans, we must abide by the rules of humans. Once we lose the desire to live as humans, we lose our worth." Therefore, we must learn the correct principles with which to live and, in essence, we must learn the meaning of character.

Intellect: "For the realization of a fuller life, it is imperative that we have and strive to develop our intelligence. Intellect aids greatly in building character."

Without a doubt, a balanced combination of the three should enable one to become a better human being.

KANO THE HUMANITARIAN

Although we have barely touched on some of his accomplishments, Dr. Kano's high ideals held a dynamic meaning which he sought to impart through the physical and spiritual activity known as judo.

For his efforts at home and abroad, the Japanese government bestowed upon Kano its highest award for humanitarianism. Dr. Kano attempted to bring about world cooperation and understanding through athletics and "large" judo activities which focused not on physical activity alone but sought to elevate the human spirit.

PRACTICAL EXPERIENCE

Reviewing the three principles or maxims of judo, relate your experiences in terms of these maxims and see where you could apply them. Write your thoughts on paper.

TEST YOURSELF

1. Describe Dr. Kano's philosophy of physical education, as it pertains to the human body, character and intellect.
2. Describe Dr. Kano's philosophy of judo as it concerns mutual welfare and benefit, maximum efficiency with minimum effort and self-perfection.3.
3. Give a brief history of the beginning of judo.
4. List some of the accomplishments of Dr. Kano.
5. Describe how judo is likened to a mountain.

True-False Questions

1. Dr. Kano believed physical education helps build the three areas of: body, character and intellect.
2. The word judo means "gentle art."
3. The first judo dojo was the *Totsuka.*
4. In his own country, Dr. Kano is honored more for his contribution to education, athletics and mankind than for his efforts in judo.
5. Dr. Kano did not approve the import of modern Western sports to Japan.
6. Judo is a means whereby one is able to find out how to use energy more effectively.
7. In the area of politics, Dr. Kano was a member of the House of Peers.
8. Although he could not speak English, Dr. Kano was a popular goodwill ambassador to the United States.
9. Dr. Kano divided judo into two types, small judo and large judo, depending on the age of the participant.
10. Dr. Kano saw judo as both a physical and spiritual activity.

Chapter XII

SOURCES OF INFORMATION

WHAT OTHER SOURCES OF
INFORMATION ARE AVAILABLE?

Books and magazines as well as other audio/visual aids provide good sources of information for expanding the student's appreciation of judo. The following is a list of possible sources. These sources are highly recommended for beginning as well as advanced students.

Books

1. *A Complete Guide to Judo*, by Smith, Robert W. Charles E. Tuttle Company. Tokyo, Japan, 1958.
2. *Foot Throws*, by Nishioka, Hayward H. Ohara Publications. Burbank, California, 1972.
3. *The Handbook of Judo*, Lebell and Coughran. Cornerstone Library. New York, 1962.
4. *Judo in Action*, Vol. 1: *Throwing Techniques*; Vol. 2: *Grappling Techniques*, Kudo, Kakuzo. Japan Publications Trading Company. Tokyo, Japan, 1967.
5. *My Championship of Judo*, Geesink, Anton. Arco Publishing Company, Inc. New York, 1966.
6. *The Mechanics of Judo*, Blanchard, Robert G. Charles E. Tuttle Company. Tokyo, Japan, 1963.
7. *The Secrets of Judo*, Watanabe, Jichi and Lindy, Avakian. Charles E. Tuttle Company. Tokyo, Japan, 1963.

8. *The Sport of Judo*, Kobayashi and Sharp. Charles E. Tuttle Company. Tokyo, Japan, 1956.
9. *Vital Judo*, Vol. 1: *Throwing Techniques*; Vol. 2: *Grappling Techniques*, Okano, Isao. Japan Publications. Tokyo, Japan, 1976.

Magazines

1. *BLACK BELT* magazine. Circulation office: 1845 W. Empire Avenue, Burbank, California 91504.
2. *Judo Journal*, Circulation office: P.O. Box 18485, Irvine, California 92713.
3. *American Judo*, Circulation office: 6417 Manchester Avenue, St. Louis, Missouri 63139. Official U.S. Judo Association publication.
4. *Judo USA*, Circulation office: 103 Harmon Gym, University of California, Berkeley, California 94720. Official U.S. Judo Federation magazine.

Films

1. *Judoka*, 16mm film lent out to schools and organizations by the Canadian Consulate, 510 W. 6th Street, Los Angeles, California 90014.
2. *Judo*, 16mm film lent out to schools and organizations by the Japanese Consulate, 250 E. 1st Street, Suite 1412, Los Angeles, California 90012.
3. *Judo Personality Daigo*, 16mm film lent out to schools and organizations by the Japanese Consulate. Same address as above.
4. *Judo Techniques*, produced and directed by Hayward Nishioka; super 8mm, designed to supplement the *Judo Textbook*. Distributed by Lowell Steiger Sports Films Company, 5224 W. Santa Monica Blvd., Los Angeles, California 90029.

PRACTICAL EXPERIENCE

Obtain a copy of two of the books mentioned above and compare their contents and approach. Using one copy of each of the magazines listed, study the different viewpoints presented.

TEST YOURSELF

1. Discuss the various strong points of each recommended book.
2. List the two recommended magazines and their selling points.

Index